In Praise of *The Novel Writer's Toolkit:*

"Whatever Bob Mayer has to tell us about writing is something we need to know. His *Toolkit* should prove an invaluable resource for beginning and seasoned writers alike. Don't miss out."
—*Terry Brooks, author of* Sometimes the Magic Works: Lessons From a Writing Life *and The Sword of Shannara trilogy*

"*The Novel Writer's Toolkit* has something for every writer, from neophyte to old hand. Using clear language, excellent organization, and many literary and commercial references, Bob Mayer looks at the process of novel writing in a way that clarifies each part of it while simultaneously trouble-shooting difficulties that are naturally inherent to this most creative of endeavors."
—*Elizabeth George, best-selling mystery novelist*

"Bob Mayer is a gifted writer and a generous teacher. This thoroughly engaging book demystifies the process of creating a novel, getting the story down, and managing the writing life. Whether you are an aspiring writer, an emerging novelist, or a published author, *The Novel Writer's Toolkit* belongs in your library. It's a book to inspire, instruct, and challenge the writer in everyone."
—*Susan Wiggs, best-selling author of* Home Before Dark

"Bob Mayer's *The Novel Writer's Toolkit* is a must-have for any writer, from *New York Times* best-selling authors to the newest newbie. I wouldn't go anywhere near a lank screen or a piece of paper without the *Toolkit* at my side."
—*Nancy Holder, author of* Blood and Fog: Buffy the Vampire Slayer

"It's much harder than it looks to be truly creative, but Bob Mayer provides an accessible and comprehensive step-by-step way to achieve it."
—*Katherine Ramsland, Ph.D., author of*
The Criminal Mind: A Writer's Guide to Forensic Psychology

Books written as Bob Mayer:

The Green Beret Way: Special Forces Tactics That Take You From Ordinary to Elite
Cut-Out
Eyes of the Hammer
Dragon Sim-13
Eternity Base
Z
Synbat

Books written as Robert Doherty:

The Rock
Area 51
Area 51: The Reply
Area 51: The Mission
Area 51: The Sphinx
Area 51: The Grail
Area 51: Excalibur
Area 51: The Truth
Area 51: Nosferatu
Psychic Warrior
Psychic Warrior: Project Aura

Books written as Greg Donegan:

Atlantis
Atlantis: Bermuda Triangle
Atlantis: Devil's Sea
Atlantis: Gate
Atlantis: Final Assault

THE
NOVEL WRITER'S
→ TOOLKIT

THE
NOVEL WRITER'S
→ TOOLKIT

A GUIDE TO WRITING NOVELS AND GETTING PUBLISHED

BOB MAYER

WRITER'S DIGEST BOOKS

Cincinnati, Ohio
www.writersdigest.com

The Novel Writer's Toolkit. Copyright © 2003 by Bob Mayer. Manufactured in the United States of America. All rights reserved. No part of this book may be reproduced in any form or by any electronic or mechanical means including information storage and retrieval systems without permission in writing from the publisher, except by a reviewer, who may quote brief passages in a review. Published by Writer's Digest Books, an imprint of F+W Publications, Inc., 4700 East Galbraith Road, Cincinnati, Ohio 45236. (800) 289-0963. First paperback edition, 2005.

Visit our Web site at www.writersdigest.com for information on more resources for writers.

To receive a free weekly E-mail newsletter delivering tips and updates about writing and about Writer's Digest products, register directly at our Web site at http://newsletters.fwpublications.com.

09 08 07 06 05   5 4 3 2 1

Library of Congress has cataloged hardcover edition as follows:

Mayer, Bob
    The Novel Writer's Toolkit: a guide to writing fiction and getting published / Bob Mayer
        p. cm.
    Includes bibliographical references and index.
    ISBN 1-58297-261-3 (alk. paper); ISBN 1-58297-320-2 (pbk: alk. paper)
        1. Fiction—Authorship. 2. Authorship—Marketing. I. Title.

PN3365.M29 2003
808'.02—dc21
                                                     2003045052
                                                        CIP

Edited by Kelly Nickell
Designed by Davis Stanard
Cover by Joanna Detz
Production coordinated by Sara Dumford

TO AIDAN MAYER

October 10, 2002

About the Author

Bob Mayer has twenty-six books published under his name and pen names including Robert Doherty and Greg Donegan. The books in his Area 51 series have been consistent *USA Today* best-sellers and have been optioned for feature film development. He has more than two million books in print and has been published in twelve foreign countries. He has taught novel writing for numerous colleges, workshops, and conferences including the Writer's Digest School. He runs a writer's retreat that focuses on the participants' work and also does corporate workshops based on his *The Green Beret Way: Special Forces Tactics That Take You From Ordinary to Elite.* Before writing full time, Bob graduated from West Point and served in the military in the Infantry and Special Forces, including command of an A-Team.

For more information visit his Web site at www.BobMayer.org.

TABLE OF CONTENTS

INTRODUCTION

This book will take you step-by-step on the entire journey from your idea, through writing your novel, to selling it, to the published book in the reader's hand, to the royalty check coming back to you. I'm going to introduce you to the skills you need to express your creativity and to increase the odds of your manuscript rising above the others languishing in the slush pile. These skills *can* be taught. Most published writing is not a special gift or a mystical talent. Writing a good novel requires hard work and can be learned, just like any other skill. It can be likened to bricklaying; you learn one brick at a time, and you get better the more bricks you lay. And you start by building a house, not a palace.

The majority of people who want to be published novelists don't want to learn anything because they think they already know all they need to know. If you are reading this, then you have already accepted that you don't know all you need to know, and therefore you are truly well ahead of the other 95 percent.

Writing is a craft, an art, and a business, and all are covered in this book.

You are going to be presented with techniques, ideas, and formats that are the "accepted" way of doing things; yet the "accepted" way makes you the same as everyone else who can read a writing book and follow instructions, and your work has to stand out from everyone else's. So how do you do that? How do you do things the "right" way, yet be different?

By using this book as a template, and allowing your creativity to grow. Think of it this way: Suppose you're a painter and this book is telling you about the paint and the canvas, lighting and perspective, and about how to sell your work to a gallery. Ultimately, you're still the one who has to decide *what* you are going to paint and *how* to paint it. This book will introduce you to the tools of writing, their advantages and disadvantages, so that you can wield them effectively.

Understand these skills, and then use your brilliance to figure out a way to change the technique or method to overcome problems and roadblocks. Learn to be original—an artist—with something that's already been done. Also learn so you can mix techniques and methods in innovative ways.

What are the basics of being a writer? First, you need to be a voracious reader. Secondly, you need to write a lot. You also need to know the writing basics: how to write in the correct perspective, use proper style and syntax, do chapter breaks, etc. Thirdly, you need to learn the proper way to do business in the world of publishing, such as the right format for a submission and how to prepare a manuscript.

The majority of writers fail because, while they may have the innate ability and drive, they lack direction and focus. That is the purpose of this book: to allow you to direct your vision into a book that others will want to buy and read.

A book comes alive in the reader's mind. You use the sole medium of the printed word to get the story from your mind to the reader's. The wonder of writing is to create something out of nothing. Every book started with just an idea in someone's head. Isn't that a fantastic concept?

Throughout these pages, I speak not only from my personal experience, but from the experience of other authors, agents, readers, teachers, and editors I have met and talked to; from reading interviews with very successful writers; and from intense study of the field of writing. I say this because I believe you can and should learn as much as possible from every source you latch onto. Take what you need and leave the rest.

If you are willing to put in the effort and the time, and become open-minded enough to recognize and understand the realities of the writing and publishing business, you will put yourself far ahead of those who believe that there is some mystical force at work with successful writers. Agents and editors read numerous cover letters where the prospective author has written something along the lines of "I hope I am lucky enough to be selected for publication." Luck comes to those who put in the sweat and blood and time.

HOW TO USE THIS BOOK

While this book is broken down into sections, they are all interconnected. Just as a good novel has many loops that tie it together, so does this book. You have to study all the pieces and all the tools that are laid out in front of you, and then try to put them together in the larger concept of not only writing a novel, but of being a professional writer.

Read through this book from start to finish. I had to decide on an order, and I decided to put the writing before the business section, but I could have just as easily, and maybe should have, put the business section first. You *must* understand the business end of writing if you wish to be published. The flow I finally decided upon was to start with you, the writer, then move forward. The more you understand where your book comes from, the better job you can do in writing it.

You'll discover that I make many links between writing your book and marketing it. There is quite a bit of overlap. The first thing you have to lock down when you start your novel is to understand yourself as a writer. Then you must come up with your one-sentence original idea. When you prepare your submission, the first sentence of your cover letter is most likely going to be that same original idea that excited you enough to write an entire manuscript. It's what your editor will use to pitch your manuscript to her publisher. It's what will go on the jacket flap of your novel. It's what will excite the reader as much as it did you. Everything is connected.

→TOOL: 1

YOURSELF

INTERNAL CHARACTERISTICS OF A WRITER

It all begins with you, the creator of your novel. It is essential that you spend some time examining yourself, much as you will examine your characters later on in the creative process. This is critical because the novel springs forth from both your intellect and your emotions.

If you wanted to become a nuclear engineer or a psychologist, you would go to college and achieve the appropriate major in four years. Then you would specialize and go to graduate school for a number of years. After school, you might have a work practicum where you could actually learn your job by doing it. Being successful in any profession requires hard work. Nevertheless, many people want to be become a published author by sitting down and writing a single manuscript and selling it. In fact, I've run into many who want to pitch their idea, get the publisher to give them a contract, and *then* write the book. It doesn't work that way. Writing is no different from any other profession. It's a simple rule, but one that every one wants to ignore: The more you write, the better you will become. Practically every author I've ever talked to, listened to, or read about in an interview, says the same thing: The most important thing to do to become a successful writer is to write a lot.

Let's look at the positive side: Most say that the odds are strongly against getting published. But simply by taking the time and the effort to read this book, you are increasing your odds. By continuing to write beyond your first manuscript, you vastly increase your odds. Many writers gush over the amount of money John Grisham made for *The Firm*, but they forget that *A Time to Kill* was published years previously to lackluster sales. What is important to understand is that Grisham realized he hadn't done something "right" in his first book, and he worked hard to change. Note that Grisham did not sit still and bemoan what his agent/editor/publisher didn't do to help the novel sell. He focused on the one factor he knew he could affect: his writing.

From talking with other published writers, you will find it is common that somewhere between manuscript numbers three and six, comes the breakthrough to being published. How many people are willing to do that much work? Not many, which is why not many succeed. On top of that, there is the fact that publishers do not often want to make a one-time investment in a writer. When a publisher puts out a book, he is backing that writer's name, and he normally wants to have more than one book in the pipeline. Currently, multiple book contracts are very common. (Their inherent advantages and disadvantages will be discussed in chapter nine.)

Not only is it hard to get published, it is also hard to be successful when you are published. Nine out of ten first novelists fail. Failure comes due to a number of reasons but the sign of it is common— enough books don't sell. I'll also discuss this in detail in chapter nine.

If you wanted to become a symphony musician, you wouldn't expect to get there the first year you picked up an instrument. Being professionally successful takes a lot of time and practice, and the best practice for a writer is writing. For novel writers, practice usually involves writing novels, although there are some very successful novelists who honed their craft writing short stories, magazine or newspaper articles, or working in Hollywood.

Read interviews with people who are successful in the arts and entertainment industries (or pretty much any profession), and you will find a common theme (with a few exceptions of course): a lot of years put in before the big "break" came. Numerous actors and comedians spent decades working in the trenches before they became famous. People seem to think that writers are different and, while in some highly publicized cases they are, most published writers have spent many years slugging away before even their first novel was published. Sue Grafton spent years writing for TV before she attempted her first novel, which was not *A Is for Alibi* and was not published. It took getting to the letter G (*G Is for Gumshoe*) in her alphabetically titled series to hit the best-seller list.

Simple perseverance counts for a lot. Many people with talent lack the drive and fall out of the picture, leaving people with maybe not as much talent but more drive to take their place. All writers go through some hard times in their writing careers. All go through times where a "normal" person would fold up shop and get a "real" job. But the successful ones don't quit even while others with more talent do. What about you?

The noted exception to this rule is celebrities who get six-figure advances for books. I know authors who are incensed over "so and so" who is a famous whatever getting a book deal. However, their book deals aren't just lucky breaks; most of these people put the time and effort into becoming well known for whatever they are well known for. The name on a book jacket sells. It's part of the business. Few people are handed success. And even if someone is successful in another field, trying to transfer their success to the writing world is still a risk—there are numerous books by celebrities that have bombed.

Something else to consider about those big advances—they can also turn into a big failure. If you get a ten thousand dollar advance and fail, no one notices much. If you get a quarter million dollars and don't earn out your advance, you can be sure everyone in the industry takes notice. Hard as it is to believe in this day of seemingly "overnight" successes, but most writers aren't overnight wonders. The majority earn their way and pay their dues with numerous manuscripts and years of learning and studying.

When your profession is writing, whether you get hired totally relies on the product—the manuscript. When you send out submissions, you are sending the end result, not the process, and it is judged as such.

Besides writing novels and reading, writers who want to be successful should attend conferences and workshops. They are worthwhile investments of your time and money, and serve as "work pracitcums." (I'll discuss this more in chapter ten.)

The other day a local college student asked me what she could do to help herself become a successful writer. I replied with my usual, "Write a lot," and then paused for a second, looking at this nineteen-year-old woman. I said, "Live a lot. Experience life, because that is what you are eventually going to be writing about."

Think about the lifestyle of an author, the lifestyle you are hoping to achieve. Most people want the end result—a published novel in the bookstore—but they don't pay much attention to the life that produces that end result. A writer's life is one of paradoxes. You have to be interested in people yet be proficient in one of the loneliest jobs there is. You need inspiration and passion, yet you must also possess the self-discipline to trudge through writing four hundred pages of a manuscript. In other words, you have to have a split personality and be slightly nuts.

I very much suggest studying the lives of writers. Read interviews with authors and see what they say. Go to conferences and talk to them. Listen to them talk about how they became authors, how they live, how they feel about writing, how they write. Many worked very strange jobs before getting published. Almost all struggled and put in years of hard work before they succeeded.

So what do you need? Briefly, you should have a large degree of all of the following:

PATIENCE AND SELF-DISCIPLINE

It will take you quite a while to finish your manuscript. Some authors work nonstop, seven days a week, when in writing mode. It *is* 99 percent perspiration and 1 percent inspiration. If you write only when excited or motivated, you'll never finish. You have to write even when it's the last thing you want to do. Just put something down. You can always edit it later or even throw it out. (You'll do a lot of throwing out. It hurts, but it's the sign of a mature writer). You may eventually average 500 to 550 pages of manuscript or more to produce 400 good pages in a final draft. To sweat over that many pages and then "lose" them hurts but not as much as getting the manuscript rejected. The more you write, the *more* you will recognize the benefits of rewriting and editing.

Additionally, the more you write, the more you will become a fan of outlining and doing a lot of work *before* you write the first sentence of your manuscript. Outlining and mapping out a novel is a trend among many authors. Both Terry Brooks and Elizabeth George got back lengthy editorial letters on the first manuscripts they sold. They both determined then and there to make sure that future manuscripts would not require such rewriting. And the manuscripts didn't. Brooks and George learned to know what they were doing before they did it. And after that, with each successive manuscript, the editorial letters became shorter and shorter.

Try to give yourself a writing goal. Write a minimum number of pages each day. Or a certain number of hours. Or a certain number of words. You can use a timer if that works for you. Ultimately, after enough manuscripts, you will develop an inner "writing clock" that will help dictate your work flow. You must be willing to force yourself to put the time and effort in, even when you don't feel like it.

While it has its benefits, being your own boss has its inherent share of problems, too. For a while, I figured if someone going to work in a factory has to punch in on a clock, why don't I? Learning how to make yourself write is something that you have to adapt to your personality. Some authors use a system of positive reinforcement. For others, keeping their inner writing clock in balance means they can actually relax and not feel guilty about not being at the keyboard. Some writers have a problem with feeling they should always be working (since they always can). You need to develop a system where you can get a lot of writing done but still take some time off and not feel guilty.

Experiment and find something that works for you in your day-to-day writing. Maybe your routine will involve writing only for one hour every morning before everyone else gets up—just keep doing it. You'll be amazed how much you can get done if you stick with it. Scott Turow wrote *Presumed Innocent* on the train to and from work in Chicago. Don't let circumstances stand in your way.

For some of you, finding undistracted time may be your greatest challenge to writing. The demands of job, family, school, whatever, can be overwhelming. And it is not so much that you can't find the time, it's that you can't find quality time. Trying to write after working ten hours at a very demanding job can be hard, but many writers manage to do it.

You have to understand yourself and how you function. How many hours in the day do you have of "good" mental time? When is your brain is working at its peak? Because even on "bad" writing days, your mind has to be working at its peak performance.

Unfortunately, there is no apprenticeship system in writing; there's no way you can make a living at it, while at the same time learning the craft. The "break point" where you can be published and get into the business is very high. This is why many people fail. There are some who do an apprenticeship writing for magazines or newspapers. In some genres this works particularly well, such as the crime reporter who ends up writing mysteries. But in most cases, such people became reporters because that's what they wanted to do, not as a stepping-stone to becoming a novelist.

When I taught martial arts, I always found that the majority of the new students quit right after the first month. They wanted to become Bruce Lee rolled into Chuck Norris all within a couple of weeks. When they realized it would take years of boring, repetitive, very hard work, the majority gave up. It doesn't take any special skill to become a black belt, just a lot of time and effort to develop the special skills. The same is true of writing. If you are willing to do the work, you will put yourself ahead of the pack. You must have long-term perspective on it. When we discuss the publishing business in the latter part of this book, I use one word to describe it: slow. Getting published requires that you, the writer, have patience.

A hard part of being a writer is knowing what exactly "work" is. For me it was hard to accept that reading a novel was work, and I wasn't being a slacker. Sitting in a coffee shop and talking with someone is work. Living itself is work for a writer in that you can only write what you know, so therefore experience is a key part of the creative process.

Ultimately, though, as the number one all-time best-selling author in Australia, Bryce Courtenay, says, you need a large dose of "bum glue": Glue yourself to that seat and write.

THE ABILITY TO ORGANIZE

As those pages pile up, you'll find yourself weeks, months, maybe years away from having written an opening chapter. That's where your organizing skills come in. You have to be aware of characters, locales, and the action, to make sure they all fit together. Try using a spreadsheet like the one found in Appendix E to create a story grid to keep track of all the relevant information. The spreadsheet is not an outline, but rather something you fill in as you write to help you remember what has been done. It helps when you need to go back and look up a specific part or change something.

In columns from left to right, the story grid has:

1. The chapter number.
2. The start page number for that chapter.
3. The end page number for that chapter.
4. The date and day of the week the action takes place on.
5. The local time.
6. The Zulu or Greenwich Mean Time equivalent of the local time— this is to keep your story in proper time sequence as it goes to various time zones. If you don't change time zones, you can place something else in this column that is applicable to your story.
7. The location of the action.
8. A brief description of the action so you can easily remember what you wrote.

You can always add a few more columns to the spreadsheet on the far right or adjust the existing ones to fit your story. You might include the real date and word or page count so you can have a record of how much work you're doing each day. Keep the story grid to the left of your keyboard as you write for easy access. Fill it in with a pencil as you add new scenes. Then every day or so enter the penciled entries into the computer and print out a new spreadsheet.

Indexed binders are an excellent way to keep research material handy and organized. I spend a considerable amount of time organizing my research material so I can find what I'm looking for. Details can drive a story, and the more research you have accessible, the more options you have in your plot.

When I discuss writing technique in chapter six, you will see where I refer to looping and tightening your subplots. The ability to organize is extremely important in keeping your story tight and fast moving.

It is interesting that something that takes you a year to produce can be "consumed" in less than a few hours. I don't even remember some of the things I wrote in my first few manuscripts, things that my readers remember very well. Since I have a series, I need to be very conscious of what I've done so far, and organization is critical for maintaining this consistency.

AN ACTIVE IMAGINATION

A novel is a living, active world you invent. Imagination is essential. In some ways, a novel is like a chess game in that you have to be able to think half-a-dozen to a dozen steps ahead for all of your pieces (characters). At the same time, you have to consider what the other guy might be doing (the limitations of your scenario and the mode/perspective chosen to present the story). You have to pick the successful moves and the correct strategic direction given a very large number of variables. But you're also limited by the personality of the characters you've invented—they have to act within the "character" you have given them, much like each chess piece is capable of only a certain type of move. It is your imagination that allows you to thread the proper path. And in most cases, there are numerous "all right" paths, but one stands out above the others as the "best" path, and finding it is critical.

I have run into a curious phenomena when people are writing what I call the memoir-novel. They are fictionalizing something that happened either to them or someone they know. When I make a suggestion to strengthen the story they'll reply, "But that's not what really happened." To which I will reply, "But it's fiction." And around and around we'll go. The advantage of fiction is that you completely can make things up. Keep your mind open to the possibilities for your story. These possibilities are where the uniqueness of your story will come out.

THE MIND

Yeah, you do sort of need one to be a writer, contrary to the opinions of some people who know me. I'd like to say a little bit more about the mind for two reasons: (1) It is ultimately the primary tool you use when writing, and (2) to write good characters, you need to understand it because it is the driving force behind your characters' actions.

As a "machine," the brain is very inefficient. Physiological psychologists estimate that we use less than 10 percent of our brain's capabilities. (Rent the Albert Brooks movie *Defending Your Life* and see how he uses this in his story.) In many ways, that is what makes writing fiction so hard and draining: You are trying to tap into the portion of your mind that you normally don't use in order to be able to touch the portion that most other people do use. A little bit of understanding of that other 90 percent is useful. It is commonly called the subconscious or the unconscious and plays a very large role in determining our own character. Whether you agree with people such as psychiatrists Sigmund Freud and Carl Jung, it is useful to know a little bit about their theories. A fully rounded character has a complete brain and, while she may only consciously be using 10 percent, that other 90 percent dramatically affects her actions.

As a writer you will start having dreams about your story and your characters. That is your mind working even when you consciously aren't. You will also run into "writer's block," which I believe, when real (vs. procrastination), is your subconscious telling you to hold until you realize in your conscious mind something important with regard to the story. This is where the "write what you feel" school of creative writing comes in. It focuses on the power of the subconscious (90 percent vs. 10 percent). Writing what you feel is more than just feeling though; it involves a large part of your brain, and the better you can get in touch with it and use it, the better your writing will be.

Writing by "feel" is hard to understand. People often ask about getting a book doctor or editor to read their work, but writers are often the best editors of their own work, if they can be objective with it. Everything that an editor or agent has pointed out that might be flawed about a manuscript I sent, I usually knew wasn't quite right before I sent it. That's not to say other readers can't help you, but a novel is ultimately the author's responsibility.

Writers should try to step outside of their own individual experiences in order to understand both their minds and the minds of other people. You have to remember that you are not the template for the rest of humanity. Hard as it may be for some to believe, there are differences between people. I've sometimes said the best thing about a writers' group is not necessarily the critiquing or networking, but rather watching the different "characters" in the group and trying to figure out what is motivating them to act the way they do.

If you don't understand yourself both mentally and emotionally, you might have a hard time understanding others. Therapy can be a very useful tool for writers to dig into their own mind to figure out where they are coming from. When I discuss what to write about in chapter three, we'll focus on a critical question writers should be able to answer: Why are you writing this novel?

While writing, it's also helpful to be aware of the two sides to the brain. The right side is your creative part while the left is more analytical and logical—the left is where the editor part of you resides. Sometimes you have to silence that editor while creating or else nothing will get done.

CONTENTMENT AND DESIRE

While wanting to make a million dollars writing isn't the most realistic of writing goals, wanting to make some money writing is a tangible reason for doing what we do. No one wants to talk about money. In the movie *White Palace,* Susan Sarandon's character is having a relationship with a younger man, and she goes with him to his apartment for the first time. She's very impressed with it and asks him how much he pays a month. He's non-plussed and hems and haws. She looks at him and says something to the effect of, "We can sleep together and make love, but you won't tell me how much you pay for your apartment?" (Her language wasn't as mild, though.) In today's society, talking about money seems more taboo than talking about sex. This taboo is particularly interesting when we consider the academic side of writing. I was sitting in a writers' group that I helped form, and we had invited a professor who edited the local university's literary publication to talk to us about the magazine. He started out by saying, "If you think you can make a living writing, forget about it."

Such negativity is damaging. You *can* make money writing. I've done it now for almost fifteen years. I've heard some authors and freelancers say never give away anything you've written for free, even if just to see it in print, and I tend to agree. If someone isn't willing to pay for it, then work harder to make it good enough so someone will. Quite honestly, most publishers will not be impressed with your credentials of getting published in publications that they never heard of and that didn't pay you anything other than to give you three free copies. That's not saying absolutely don't do it, but if you do, realize such publications are only a step and you need to move beyond them. Don't get stuck there. Such publications are especially prominent with the growth of the Internet. There's plenty of places you can "post" your writing, but they haven't yet replaced getting published.

I am not saying to write simply for the money, but if you don't factor money into the writing equation somewhere, and take it as a serious factor, you will fail, because eventually you will have to get a "real" job. It's a vicious equation: To become a better writer, you must write. To write you must have time to write. To have time to write, it most certainly helps to make some money at it.

In a perfect world I suppose we could accomplish all the things we would like without having a external stimulus like money. But this isn't a perfect world. For additional motivation, I often find putting my back against the wall helps. I wrote my first two novels living in Korea. I studied and taught martial arts six hours a day and went nuts the rest of the time. I wrote, to a certain extent, to keep my sanity. Then after getting published, I wrote because I enjoyed it, but also to make money to live on. I had job offers where I could be financially secure, but I didn't take them. I wrote, and continue to write, because I have to both internally and externally.

Okay, now that we've gotten the mercenary side of the business out of the way, let's go back to the passion that is absolutely necessary to survive—and thrive—in this profession. Some people tend to look down upon telling a story in a format such as science fiction or mystery or action/adventure. But if that's your passion and your story, then tell it and don't worry about what anyone thinks. There is one bottom line on how good a writer is, and that's how many people read his book. Such writing is called "commercial" writing and sneered at in certain quarters, but if no one wants to read what a person writes then maybe he just isn't writing that well. Think about it.

I've said that to become a writer, you must write. It is critical to understand the business aspects of publishing and marketing your work as best you can, but I have seen people (including myself at times) forget one other very important rule: You have to have a good product. You can be the greatest marketing specialist in the world, but if you don't have a product people want to read, you're not going to get published. Putting 90 percent of your effort into trying to sell your work when it is simply not good enough is a waste of time. Put that effort into writing another manuscript that *is* good enough.

I sat on a panel at a conference once, and the moderator asked each of us what we liked and disliked about writing for a living. The answers were interesting. An author needs the paradoxical combination of being able to be content and discontent at the same time. Because publishing is such a slow business and positive feedback so rare, you have to be reasonably content for long periods of time by yourself. At the same time you have to motivate yourself to write the manuscript, to do all the dirty work that needs to be done, and to pursue long-range goals.

SETTING OBJECTIVES

So far I've talked about what you need. Now let me mention something we could all do without: procrastination. If you're like me, when you were in school that term paper never really got done until the night before it was due. (In fact, the one time I did write a paper early—so early, in fact, that I was able to get feedback before officially turning it in—I got an F. So much for positive reinforcement.)

The best way to overcome procrastination is to decide upon both short- and long-term objectives. For the short-term, set a daily objective of a minimum number of pages to write or a certain number of hours a day at the keyboard. If researching, give yourself a goal of perhaps a book a night to be looked through and summarized.

For your long-term objectives, print out a calendar about once a week with the next twelve months on it. Block out every known appointment, and then break it down by writing projects. Block out weeks and months to write, outline, or edit a certain book. Make weekly writing goals that you can break down into your daily goals. Post that long-term calendar by your workspace. You also might want to keep an erasable board on hand. On it, list everything you have to do that day (including hours of writing, phone calls to be made, things to be mailed, etc.). As you accomplish each task, wipe it off the board. At the end of the day, if something is left up there, not only have you not accomplished what you should have, but it's still up there for the next day. Since you're your own boss, it is very easy to slip up, but with your time objectives sitting there on a board, less than four feet from your nose, it becomes a little harder.

If you feel such cold objectives interfere with your creativity, you might be right. But a novel is a hell of a long way to go simply burning the fuel of passion. Many people start a novel, get about a quarter of the way in, then drop it to move on to a "better" idea. In everything I've worked on, about a hundred and fifty pages in, my mind has already started to move on to a new project, and I'm somewhat bored with what I am working on. That's where discipline and a schedule come in. If my next project isn't due to start for three more months, then I have to work those three months on my present project in order to earn the right to start the new one.

WRITER'S BLOCK

I decided to discuss the evergreen problem of writer's block after objectives because if you're experiencing it, you have to decide whether your creative juices have run dry or if you are committing the sin of procrastination. On the whole, I have to honestly say most often when I grind to a halt, I am doing the latter.

Ways to overcome the "block":

1. Have a good outline. Since you've already poured a lot of creativity into your outline, you can usually keep going.

2. Just write anyway. It might be awful, but at least you're left with something other than a blank page. You'll be surprised how little difference there is between what you write when you feel motivated and what you write when you're discouraged. They both come from the same brain.

3. Work on another project for a while. Looking up at my work board now, I have:

   A. One manuscript on the market with a publisher.

   B. One partial manuscript/concept with an agent, looking for representation.

   C. A screenplay getting read by a producer for rewrite.

   D. Two concepts for third books, to follow two two-book contracts with major publishers, that need to be outlined in time for a new contract.

   E. Two new ideas that I'm researching and beginning to outline.

   F. Two manuscripts getting edited at publishing houses and due back in the next month for more work.

You should have plenty of other things you can focus on for a short period of time while you try to rejuvenate your creativity. One way to do that is cycle back to the research stage of the creative process. (We'll discuss research more in chapter four.) Since details drive your story, look for more details in your research.

Another option is to go back and, with an open mind, reread what you've already written, looking for subconscious seeds you've planted but haven't harvested. (You'll find more on this in the section on subplots in chapter six.)

4. If you are sure that you need to pause to rethink where your novel is heading, give the writing you have so far to someone for feedback. Talk to additional people. Clear you head. Free-associate. Turn everything in your novel around and look at it from another perspective. Scream. Pound your forehead into your keyboard. Then write.

OPEN-MINDEDNESS

You could also call open-mindedness the "willingness to change." Not only is it important when starting out, but open-mindedness is vital after first getting published. You should be willing to continuously learn from any source to improve your writing.

Before you can be willing to change though, you have to be willing to say three of the hardest words in the human language: "I was wrong." This should be followed with: "Maybe I'm not doing this the best possible way. Maybe I can learn from someone else."

Too many writers want validation instead of help. They want to be told how great their manuscript is and have a publisher put the check in the mail. They don't want to hear what's wrong and what additional work needs to be done. After I had three books published, I took some graduate literature courses at my local college to expand my horizons. In fact, the longer I write, the more I appreciate the literary side of the craft. I think many genre writers get too caught up in the "formula" of their genre and trap themselves, becoming unable to write anything different. In the same manner, if you have a background in literature, don't turn your nose up at information that seems too "common" or genre oriented.

I recently watched a visiting writer at a local college come into our writers' group to do a reading. She walked in, gave her reading, took her applause, and then walked out. She didn't take the time to find out whom she had just read to and because of that she lost the opportunity to network with several published authors who might have helped *her* in her attempts to publish her next novel.

Keep in mind that you never know who you're dealing with, so be courteous and open to all you meet. No matter what your mind-set, listen to others and what they have to say about writing, even if you disagree with them. You might find yourself agreeing a year or two later. In this book, you might find me to be somewhat schizo-phrenic, taking several different perspectives, some of them seemingly opposed to each other. But remember, I began writing this in 1990 and have been adding to it ever since, so in these pages you see some of my evolution as a writer. When I first started out, I was very touchy, for mainly egocentric reasons, at what I perceived to be "snubs" from the literary community toward genre writing. Now I simply see that attitude to be naive and wrong. You have to decide what *you* want to do and pursue it, regardless of what others say or believe. It's also important to remember that someone, somewhere, will not like what you've written after you get published. It's also guaranteed that some of those people will feel a burning desire to inform you of those dis-likes. By staying open-minded, you'll be able to take such comments with a grain of salt.

The biggest change I have made over the years is to adjust my perspective on plotting and characters. I will discuss this in further detail in chapter six, but for my first dozen manuscripts or so, I be-lieved that the plot drove the story. Now I try to let the characters drive the story. In order to make that change, though, I had to admit that what I was doing was not the best way to work and be willing to look at points of view diametrically opposed to my own.

You can't ever get better if you don't first admit you're not doing it the best possible way. When I taught a writing correspondence course, I would have to say that 90 to 95 percent of the students were unwilling to change anything based on the feedback I was giving them. I wondered why they even took the course in the first place. The answer, as I mentioned above, is that they wanted validation. The few who did change, who reworked their material and put the time into thinking about the questions I would posed, made great strides as writers.

Open-mindedness also comes into play in the business side of the craft. Too often, new writers want to do things *their* way and expect editors, agents—the entire publishing community—to see everything the same way as they do. Frankly, that doesn't happen. There are many things wrong in the business, but there are also many things right. And just because *you* might not see the reason why certain things are the way they are, that doesn't make them wrong.

Remember, also, that change comes in stages. First one has to accept that there is a need for change. Then you have to intellectually accept the change, which isn't total acceptance. After a while of living with the mental acceptance, you will gradually have emotional acceptance of the change, which is total acceptance. That is why it takes years and years to change, if one ever does.

To keep a fresh and open mind, it's good to read a wide range of books. I especially recommend that new novelists read two types of books: first novels (because these books are sold on their own merits), and breakout novels (these books transform midlist authors into bestselling authors).

THE WRITING ROUTINE

People always want to know what a writer's "routine" is. I get that question when I teach, and I have a hard time answering it. My standard reply is that I will use and do whatever it takes to get a manuscript done. If I have to outline on an easel pad, I'll do it. If I have to write in chalk on the side of an apartment building, I'll do it. If I have to call the homicide squad to ask a stupid question, I'll try to get someone else to do it, and when they won't, I'll do it myself.

Each individual has to discover what works, but the operative word in this sentence is *work*. Don't lock yourself in—find what works, and if it stops working, find something else.

While your approach to writing needs to be individualized to your needs, at heart, it's probably very similar to those of other writers. I once listened to a panel where authors Terry Brooks, Elizabeth George, Bryce Courtenay, and Dan Millman talked about their own writing processes. On the surface it appeared that all were very different in their approach. However, underlying each approach was essentially the same principles, they were just carried out differently. Confusing? For example, Terry Brooks is a big fan of outlining and hates rewriting. But Bryce Courtenay doesn't outline, he just starts writing and then spends a lot of time rewriting. In essence, Bryce Courtenay's first draft of the manuscript is equal to Terry Brooks polished outline. The same thought processes and amount of work go into each.

PASSION

Passion is what *you* feel about the story you're writing, and it will come through in your writing, both consciously and subconsciously. (I talk about intent—what you want the reader to get from the book—in chapter three.) Your passion might be to tell an interesting and entertaining story. It could be to write a novel about what love means to you. Sometimes when I am trying to get a writer to get back to her original idea, I ask her what she believes is most important about her book. What does she care the most for? The originating emotion is the core of the book.

When it comes to selling your book, it's essential for you to be able to relay your passion to the agent or editor. Something excited you when you began writing your book, and you need to excite others in the same way with the finished product.

I've seen writers totally change their manuscripts based on a single offhand comment from an editor, agent, or writing instructor. Sometimes the change is for the better, but sometimes it tears the heart out of the book.

A writer has to be true to herself first. But the writer also must be objective enough to get out of her own head and see if what she has written works. She needs to balance feedback and criticism with her own goals and desires for the writing. To have these capabilities reside inside of one person is a paradox. But when these paradoxes are in balance, a writer is able to write and sell their work successfully.

→ TOOL: 2

YOUR SURROUNDINGS

TOOLS FOR DAY-TO-DAY WRITING

Like any other profession, there are tools the writer uses. Here are some you should consider:

COMPUTERS AND WORD PROCESSORS

Tolstoy's wife copied six drafts of *War and Peace* in freehand for him as he wrote it. Since most of us aren't as lucky to have such an understanding spouse or friend, a computer or word processor is almost indispensable. I salute those legions of writers who produced their works before the day of electronic "cut" and "paste."

Prices for computers have come down considerably over the last several years. I recently bought a computer with a hard drive that cost less than half of what the same make computer (with no hard drive) cost me eight years ago. You don't need anything fancy, just something that will work and crunch words. (Note: If you can't afford one or it just isn't practical, you can usually get access to a computer at a local university or library.)

Laptops are also handy. A laptop works the same way as a regular desktop computer, but it can give you much more flexibility. You can take it to the library to do research; you can bring it on trips or to your job, or you can work while you commute. I just purchased an adapter for my laptop that plugs into the cigarette lighter in my car, allowing me to charge my battery while on the road and increasing my working capability. I haven't yet learned the trick of writing while driving (I'm not sure I will accomplish that feat), but I have been known to tap out thoughts and ideas at rest areas.

I used to do quite a few book signings at military post exchanges throughout the country. These signings consisted of sitting in front of the post exchange for twelve hours at a time and trying to sell my books. I spent a lot of that time at the keyboard of my laptop, tackling two jobs at once.

For writing, you probably need at least a word processor. There are what I would call "upgraded" typewriters on the market now that carry out the same functions without the expense of a computer. They work well, too. Basically the machine you use should have the ability to store your words and allow you to rework them through editing, cutting, and pasting electronically. In fact, most computers are much more powerful than what you need (capable of making phone calls, balancing your household budget, exploring on the Internet, doing the laundry, and a whole list of other tasks). All you need is something with a keyboard that will allow you to save what you write.

Always back up your work. And do it often. Nothing is more agonizing than to lose pages you have just written because of a mechanical malfunction or a power loss. When I was writing my first couple of manuscripts in Korea, the power would cut out at the strangest times, and I learned to automatically hit the keys for save at the end of pretty much every paragraph. Most current word processing programs have an automatic save that you can set.

Keep the latest copy of what you're writing on your hard drive and back it up on disk every day. Every week save the backup onto another disk, which you can leave in your car. You never know, your home may catch on fire and the computer and home backup disk may be destroyed. Paranoid? Slightly, but I know there's someone out there who lost everything when they thought it was safe.

Someone might ask, "Can't I simply write on a legal pad with a pencil?" Certainly, if that's what you prefer. Joyce Carol Oates writes her first draft with pen and paper. Some authors dictate their stories onto a microcassette recorder and then transcribe it. You should choose whatever works best for you. I'm simply suggesting a word processor as the easiest way for most people.

I once met someone at a writers conference who wrote his manuscripts out in longhand and then gave them to a typist. He bemoaned the fact that he couldn't afford to buy a computer. I had to point out to him that the amount of money he paid the typist for one manuscript was half the purchase price of a computer.

PRINTERS

Spend the extra money for a LaserWriter or inkjet printer. You need letter quality for manuscripts you're submitting. Many publishers won't even look at a dot matrix manuscript. If you've ever tried reading a manuscript printed on dot matrix you'll understand why. While laser print cartridges can be expensive, they ultimately cost less per page than buying ribbons for a dot matrix. Also, you can recharge laser cartridges, which can save you money and is environmentally sound.

As great as all this equipment can be, never let it stand in the way of your writing. Lincoln once wrote a nice piece of prose on the back of an envelope on the way to a place called Gettysburg. Of course, as we will discuss in the second half of this book, if he had tried submitting it in that format to a major New York publisher or agent, he wouldn't have made it out of the slush pile. Well, actually, Lincoln, as President, would have. You and I wouldn't have.

A PLACE TO WRITE

The ideal writing place for one person can be a completely different environment than that of another. I like quiet most of the time, while others may want music playing in the background. Some writers may prefer to write in solitude, others may prefer to work in the presence of another dedicated writer.

My work area has expanded over the years. Currently, I have a wraparound desk with more than nine feet of length, a large four-drawer file cabinet, two windowsills full of books, five steel shelves holding various materials, two ceiling-high bookcases, several vertical files, two cork bulletin boards, a dry-erase board, etc. When I write, I need plenty of area, and I like to keep my work as organized as possible.

Some people like to grab a pencil and notepad, and curl up in bed. Others climb a mountain and write on the peak. Again, whatever works best and is within your realm of possibilities. I'm writing this paragraph sitting behind two card tables at a book signing I'm doing at the post exchange in Fort Rucker, Alabama. As you can tell, I don't exactly have a line of people waiting to buy books, but I'm using the time to my advantage and not worrying that I'm not sitting at home behind my desk.

A MASTER CHARACTER LIST

A master character list provides you with quick descriptions and personal histories for each person in your book. Every time you use a name, write it down and give a brief description of the character, even if you think it is someone you will never use again in the manuscript. This will spare you from losing time, searching back, looking for the name of that minor character that you used somewhere in the first hundred pages and who suddenly, unexpectedly, reappears in chapter twenty-three. It helps considerably to have the character work done *prior* to starting the novel—more on this in chapter six.

Another good reason to keep track: You won't slip up and use the same name for a different character in the course of writing.

In a similar way, write down any key fact you make up or use so you can remember it.

MAPS OF LOCALES

If you can't stay oriented, your reader can't either. When I read *Lonesome Dove*, I had my atlas at my side and followed the herd from the Mexico-Texas border all the way up north to Montana. As an author, you have to do the same thing. As I look about my office, I see, all within handy reach:

>> *Rand McNally Universal World Atlas*
>> *The Times Atlas of World History*
>> *The Hammond Universal World Atlas*
>> *Rand McNally 2003 Road Atlas of the United States*
>> *Rand McNally Road Atlas of Europe*
>> *Atlas of Earth Mysteries*
>> *Atlas of the Second World War*
>> *The West Point Atlas of American Wars*
>> A Michelin map of "Africa: Central and South; Madagascar." (This is for a book I'm currently working on.)
>> A Xeroxed copy of a geographic map of a section of the Rocky Mountains (again for a specific project).

I just bought a two hundred dollar atlas at my local bookstore because I have found maps to be critical to my stories. I always end up looking up very strange and rare places. Know where Ngorongoro Crater is? I'm using it in my next book, and I didn't know where it was either until I tracked it down in an atlas.

Not only do these atlases and maps give you locales, they give histories and facts about the locales that often become essential to the story. When I get down and dirty in an action scene, I use topographic maps to give me a feel for the terrain. Maps are also useful in determining distances (remember people do take time to travel—unless of course you're writing science fiction in which case). Make sure your rules work and remain consistent within the covers of the book when your spaceship hits warp drive.

There are certain genres where maps are very important. If you've ever read The Lord of the Rings trilogy you know where the Shire is in relation to Mordor, and you know about the land in between. If you write historical fiction, your readers might want to know what the political boundaries of the time were.

Also, and I shudder to mention this, there are people who don't exactly know where, let's say, Madagascar, is.

When I was in Special Forces we did what we called an "area study" before we went to another country. We spent time learning everything we could about the place: topography, weather, customs, languages, religions, etc. As a writer, I do the same thing before I write about a place.

DIAGRAMS OF IMPORTANT PLACES

Diagrams, like maps will help to keep you oriented as you write. If you can't stay oriented, your reader certainly won't be able to. If your main character turns left into the bedroom for the first fifteen chapters and you make a mistake and have her turn right in chapter sixteen, there is no doubt but that it will be noticed. With books, the reader can always turn back and check your information.

A DICTIONARY

Yes, I have seen cover letters with words misspelled. Over the last several years, I've learned that although I may think I know what a word means, occasionally I am wrong. Sometimes it pays to look it up and know exactly what you are saying.

A friend of mine left a store, walked to her convertible, and found a note stuck on her windshield. A guy who had been eyeing her in the store left it. She opened it up and read, along with his phone number, the words, "Let's meat."

Needless to say they didn't meat. Spelling is important.

A STORY GRID

As I discussed earlier, a story grid, like the one in Appendix E, keeps you oriented and allows you to go back and find certain passages quickly, rather than rereading the entire manuscript. For the type of stories I write, it is extremely important to be able to keep track of location, time, characters, and action. For example, remember that there's a fourteen hour time difference between Washington and Tokyo, so your hero can't fly between the two in thirty minutes (unless you're writing science fiction, of course).

While a story grid may not seem like the most artistic thing in the world, it's very important. While writing is a creative task, a novel requires quite a bit of organizational ability, and sometimes it is difficult to be both creative and organized. Once you start it—and I will go into this in more detail in chapter five—the story takes on a life of its own and in a paradoxical manner, your creativity is limited by your creation growing on its own.

The story grid is not an outline. You should fill it in as you write so you can keep track of what you've already done. It is particularly helpful when rewriting. As you will see when we get to subplots, when you change one aspect of a novel, it tends to have a ripple effect and change things in other places. It's easier to realize and find these other places using the story grid.

You can also compare your story grid to your outline as you progress and see how close the two are. This will keep you from going too far astray from the story you planned to write.

SUMMARIES OF IMPORTANT INFORMATION

You should summarize research articles and books, writing the important information (along with the source and page numbers) with bullets that you can quickly scan. When your story stalls out, look through the bulleted pages of information to remind yourself of some piece of information that might allow you to rejuvenate the story line. Remember that class on research that you had in school so many years ago? The same principles apply to writing fiction.

Details drive a story, and the more information you have, the more details you have. Large sections of some of my books are based on facts that readers think are fiction. Other writers may create a fictional history for a fact.

NEWSPAPER AND MAGAZINE ARTICLES

You can take any newspaper and come up with two or three book ideas from the front page. Newspapers and magazines can also give you great background information. Articles in particular do a lot of the research for you by summarizing information. Index excerpts and place them in three ring binders for handy reference. The information might be fresh in your mind when you read the article, but five months from now, when you're in the middle of writing chapter twenty-seven, you'll be lucky if you can even remember reading the article, never mind what was in it—writing a novel is a *long* process. To have the article on hand allows you to access the material quickly and efficiently.

DVDS AND VIDEOTAPES

When I was writing *The Rock* about Ayers Rock in Australia, I was writing about a place I'd never visited. I did not have the funds or the time to fly to Australia to research an idea that I had not sold, so I did the next best thing. I rented travel videos and toured the country via my TV. I was able to sit at my desk and describe scenes as I watched them. Of course I didn't have the actual feel of the place, but I could gain additional information by researching travel accounts of people who *had* been there. Ask around—you'll be amazed at the number of people in your neighborhood who've gone to the strangest places.

You can learn about firearms, medical procedures, bungee jumping, hang gliding, and more—all from electronic media. Naturally it is best to actually go to the locales or to do the action yourself so you can write about it accurately, but when that isn't possible, videos and DVDs can be the next best thing.

INDEXED BINDERS

Binders can hold your essential information so you can find whatever factoid you want whenever you need it. Having stacks of information that aren't organized does you little good.

A MICROCASSETTE RECORDER

A microcassette recorder can be helpful to remember thoughts when you're driving or in a position where you can't easily write. Keep it by the side of your bed at night so that when you wake at three in the morning with that brilliant idea, you can mutter it into the recorder and play it back in the morning when your cognitive functioning is somewhat restored.

A LARGE EASEL PAD

Try putting your outline on a large easel pad and filling it in as you write. The large page allows you to record more and is especially useful if you are visually oriented when you think of a story. You can scrawl notes all over the large space and refer back to it more easily than if you had twenty smaller sheets of 8½" by 11" paper.

BOOKS

As I've discussed earlier, to be a successful writer you have to be well read. Not only that, but as you will see when we get to the research chapter, other fiction novels can often be good sources for not only facts, but techniques of writing that you will find helpful. Whatever problem you run into, the odds are some writer in the past ran into the same problem—how did they solve it? Then, being the brilliant person you are, you have to figure out a better way.

Just a few weeks ago, I spent a week reading the current fifteen *New York Times* best sellers. I did this because I want to write a *New York Times* best seller. I read the books with an open mind, and I picked up some valuable techniques. I adjusted some of the structure of my plotting in accordance with what I learned. Other people's writing can help you improve your own.

→TOOL: 3

YOUR IDEA

WHAT TO WRITE

Mark Twain said, "Write what you know." I have four addendums to that:

1. I like to rephrase it to: "Write what you know *and feel something about.*"
2. You will most likely write something in the same area of the books you like to read.
3. Understand that some of what you know and feel something about, other people might not be particularly interested in, especially if they know the same things you do. Unless, of course, your book is written in a superlative manner.
4. You can also write about *what you want to know.* Elizabeth George writes best-selling mysteries based in England, and she

lives in California. I write about myths and legends because they interest me, and I'm willing to do the research to learn more. I believe that if I can find material that interests me, I can find readers it interests.

Usually your background and knowledge will dictate what your story is about. That's not to say that since you haven't ever gone into space that you can't write science fiction, but it does mean that you need to know something about the physics of space flight if that is going to be in your manuscript. As you will see later, when it comes to marketing your manuscript you are also marketing yourself. Even more than your background, your reading tastes will affect what you write about. You will most likely write whatever it is you enjoy reading. The best preparation for becoming a writer of mysteries is to have read a lot of mysteries.

Some words of advice here: Start with something simple. Don't try to write the Great American Novel on your first try. You'll find that you're constantly learning more about writing and polishing your skills every time you write. As you learn more, you can write more difficult plots and more complex characters.

And now some further words of caution. I've said you should write what you know and you should keep it as simple as possible, but be careful. A common problem with new writers is the misguided belief that *their* life story will be extremely interesting to the reading world—the fictional memoir I discussed earlier. As I said in my third addendum to Mark Twain's saying, there is nothing inherently wrong with writing about yourself, but be realistic about the possibilities of someone else wanting to read it.

Writing about a subject you care about very deeply has the advantage of adding passion to your prose. The disadvantage is that some writers can't separate themselves enough from what they write to adequately judge its content or style. I have watched writers waste *years* on the same manuscript, trying to polish the editing, doing rewrites on various subplots, etc., when they were not willing to accept a fundamental problem with their story: The basic idea wasn't working or wasn't that interesting.

Many writers become too emotionally attached to bad ideas. As I mentioned earlier, open-mindedness is a very important trait for writers. In chapter seven, I've devoted a section to the reader. The reason? Too many writers get tunnel vision and fail to objectively evaluate their own work in terms of someone who has no emotional attachment and is seeing it for the first time. Just because you feel something doesn't mean you can get the reader to feel the same thing.

The problem any writer faces when approaching his first manuscript is that he is trying to do something new. Most wise people, when trying to do something new, use the KISS technique (keep it simple, stupid). Any time you write, you're trying to juggle two glass balls: the story and the writing. The simpler you make the story, at least as you're starting out, the more attention you can give to the writing.

That sounds rather simplistic, but many writers get in over their heads by trying to write a very complex first novel, and the writing suffers as they wrestle with the story. Most first novelists can do one or the other well, but very few can do both well. Since you must write well, give yourself a break on the story. When I was still unpublished and got hooked up with an agent, his first (and only) comment to me was to simplify the plot of the manuscript I submitted. I had too much going on in my story and was not a skilled enough writer to keep it all going. I did as he suggested, and that book was the first one we sold.

In fact, I've come full circle. I've written a couple of series of books that have done well (Area 51, Atlantis) but are very complicated, with a large cast of characters and complex story lines that generally rewrite the entire history of mankind. Talk about difficult. I've also written some thrillers that were quite complicated. The next book I write that's not under contract is going to feature a very simple idea and story line where I can focus on giving my characters the depth I usually devote to the plot.

One thing to be careful of: Often the first book a person writes is an expunging of personal demons. Thus it holds great emotional weight for the writer but it might not do the same for the reader. This is another reason you should start your second novel immediately afterwards.

Another problem to beware of: perfectionism. Some people think that the writing has to be perfect. They spend an inordinate amount of time editing and rewriting. Sometimes, you just have to accept it's either good enough, or that the horse is dead and can't be brought back to life.

I am going to stay on my soapbox a little bit longer. I just finished looking at a couple dozen novel submissions for a contest I am judging. I have yet to see one that was not about love, death, divorce, child abuse, broken hearts, etc. Nobody said, "Hey, I've got a great science fiction story here." Or a horror story. Or a thriller. There's nothing wrong about writing about love, death, etc., but none of the writers whose manuscripts I reviewed were up to the task.

Now, here's an easy exercise: Go to the bookstore and look around. What is the largest section? In the bookstores I frequent, the largest is computers. Second largest? Self-help. Ah, what is self-help about? Love, death, addiction, child abuse, broken hearts, etc. Last I checked, it was nonfiction.

Remember why people read fiction: We read it to escape death, abuse, addiction, broken hearts, etc. We read primarily to be entertained. Yet, many aspiring writers try to write The Great American Novel—one that features the very subjects readers want to escape. How many of these Great American Novels are on the bookshelves? Maybe 10 to 20 percent of the hardcover new releases. Less than 10 percent of the paperback original releases. You figure it out.

I really believe that the number one problem most new novelists have is picking very difficult subject matter for their story. The craft of writing is difficult enough. The more difficult the topic is, the better the writing has to be.

You need to have an original thought or idea that will spark your passion and that of others.

THE ORIGINAL IDEA

The original idea is the foundation of your novel. When I say idea, I don't necessarily mean the theme or the most important incident, although both could be the original idea. The original idea can be a setting. It can be a scene. It can be a character.

Your original idea is simply the first idea you had that is the seed of your novel. All else can change, but the idea can't. It might be a place, a person, an event, a moral, whatever. But you had it before you began writing and you *must* remember it as you write. If you don't, your story and style will suffer terribly. You should be able to tell your idea in one sentence. And repeat it to yourself every morning when you wake up and prior to writing. Knowing it will keep you on track.

Here's a quick test: Write down the original idea for your book in *one* sentence.

If you can't do it, then you need to backtrack through your thought processes to find it, because you had to have had it. Everything starts from something. While the original idea is not the story, something I'll talk about more later, it is the one thing in your manuscript that cannot change.

So, the above isn't very clear? Okay. In one of my early novels, the original idea was an action: What if Special Forces soldiers had to destroy an enemy pipeline? That's it for *Dragon Sim-13*. Not very elaborate, you say. True. Not exactly a great moral theme. Right. But with that original idea there was a lot I could do and eventually had to do. I had to change the target country after the first draft. But that was okay because I still had the original idea. I had to change characters, but that was fine too, because it didn't change my original idea. I had to change the reason *why* they were attacking a pipeline, but again, okey-dokey because, you got it, the original idea was the same.

Allan Folsom, who received a two million dollar advance for his first novel, *The Day After Tomorrow*, said it all began with an idea: What if a man sitting in a Paris café sees someone who had played a significant role in his earlier life but whom he hadn't seen in twenty years?

Think of all the possibilities that simple idea allows, but also think of the starting point it gives you. He doesn't say who it was the man sees. He doesn't even say why the man is in Paris in the first place. Heck, he doesn't even say who the man is. Is he a spy? A tourist? The plot in *The Day After Tomorrow* ended up having someone carrying Hitler's head around in a case.

You will have plenty of latitude after you come up with your original idea; in fact, you may find the finished manuscript turns out to be different from what you had originally envisioned, but one thing is always true: That original idea is still there at the end.

I made my original idea for my first manuscript as simple as possible for me to write; when I was in the Special Forces, my A-Team *had* run a similar mission on a pipeline. Since I had a good idea of what would happen in the story, I could concentrate on the actual writing of the novel. It needed every bit of that concentration, and even then was barely readable.

I've sat in graduate literature classes and heard students say: "The author had to have a moral point in mind when she wrote that book." I agree, but sometimes it is not at the forefront of the story. Many authors write simply to tell a story started by their original idea, which indeed might be a moral point, but sometimes the actual theme develops *during* the writing, not before.

After you have that original idea, you should spend a lot of time wrestling with it and developing some feelings and thoughts about it. Try to look at your main characters and determine what will happen to them emotionally, physically, and spiritually as they go through the story. Who are they at the beginning of the story? Who are they at the end?

Such questioning helps you become aware of what you are doing. While not all authors have a conscious theme in mind when they write a novel, experience has taught me that it is better to have it in mind before you start writing. It might not be your original idea, but it will definitely affect your characters and story. Readers want to care about the story and the characters they discover in a book. If there is a moral or emotional relevance to the story, readers will become emotionally involved, and will enjoy the story more. And readers might not even consciously see the theme either.

Using the "what if" technique can be very helpful in clarifying your original idea, and also, as we will see later, when you write your cover letter and synopsis for submission.

"What if a housewife realizes her life is empty and decides to change it?" Not very specific you might argue, but the specifics will come out later. You have the original idea that will allow you to drive from a start to a finish.

John Saul and Mike Sack at the Maui Writers Conference run a seminar called "what if?" They ask writers to write their one sentence idea on butcher paper, and then they analyze it. They make sure every word in the sentence means something. For example: What if Mary has to stop a band of terrorists?

How could this be improved? Who is Mary? How about "a housewife"?

Stop a band of terrorists from what? How about "assassinating the president"?

This gives us: What if a housewife has to stop a band of terrorists from assassinating the President?

Do you see how much stronger the second "what if" is, how many more story possibilities it produces?

Sometimes the original idea could even be a way to tell a story. Telling the same story from two different perspectives usually presents two different stories. For example, take the original idea, "What if a person with limited mental capacity interacts with the world?" The film *A Dangerous Woman* (films work the same way) shows normal, everyday life with the main character being a woman who always tells the truth. Boy, you want to talk about someone who is dangerous. Think about it. The film is an excellent portrayal of society, but the original idea was the different perspective. What was *Forrest Gump* about? It had the same basic "what if?" Wasn't it the main character's perspective rather than the actual events that made the story?

A different point of view can be a way to tell a story that's already been done in a fresh way. In *Beowulf*, the reader doesn't hear the monster's story—it took John Gardner to tell it later in *Grendel*. Who was the madwoman in the attic in *Jane Eyre*? She had her story, and Jean Rhys told it in *Wide Sargasso Sea*. Jane Smiley put *King Lear* on a present day farm and called it *A Thousand Acres*.

Whenever you read a book or watch a movie, try to figure out the original idea the first screenwriter had. For example, in the movie *True Romance* written by Quentin Tarantino, there is a scene at the end where four groups of people in a room are all pointing guns at each other in a classic Mexican standoff. Rewatching the film, I can imagine the mind of a writer driving the entire movie to that one climactic scene. In an interview, Tarantino said that scene was the original idea when he started. He didn't know who the people with the guns were (characters); where the room was (setting); why they were in the room (plot); whether it was the beginning, end or middle of the movie (pacing of the story); what the result of this standoff would be (climactic scene); etc. He just had this first (original) vision.

Here are a few examples of how the "what if" question has assisted me in developing my own story ideas:

>> What if people going into the witness protection program really disappear? *Cut-Out.* I came up with this idea after watching *Goodfellas* with some friends and began wondering about what really happened to people who were no longer needed by the government to testify.

>> What if the force that destroyed Atlantis ten thousand years ago comes back and threatens our world? The Atlantis series of books. I'd always been fascinated with myths and legends, and decided to translate one of the oldest myths to present day.

>> What if we didn't originate the way we think we did? The Area 51 series. It struck me that both sides of the creationist vs. evolutionist argument might be wrong. So what was a third option?

>> What if Japan succeeded in its atomic bomb program at the very end of World War II, and one of those bombs is now hidden at the base of the Golden Gate Bridge? *The Gate.* I was wandering in the library one day and saw a book called *Japan's Secret War.* Curious, I pulled it off the shelf and began reading. The author claimed that he had evidence the Japanese actually developed two atomic bombs at the end of World War II and detonated a test bomb in the waning days of the war in Manchuria. As a fiction writer, I realized this was something I could develop into an exciting, present-day thriller.

Original ideas, especially for genre books, should be exciting. How about this: *Jaws* meets *Jurassic Park*? That was the idea behind Steve Alten's blockbuster novel, *Meg*, published in 1997. Combining two great ideas into something new is a technique many best-selling writers use.

At conferences and workshops, I often ask writers, "Why did you write this book?" Writers tend to get lost among the trees once they enter the forest that's a novel. They forget why they started the journey in the first place. Something excited you at the very beginning, enough that you ended up sitting down and writing thousands upon thousands of words. What was it?

Another way to try to figure out the core of your novel is by asking yourself, "What serves as the climactic scene?" The climactic scene is when the protagonist and antagonist meet to resolve the primary problem that is the crux of the novel.

As I mentioned earlier, the original idea is not necessarily the theme of the book. It can be, but the two are not necessarily synonymous. And if they aren't the same, you should know what your theme is anyway.

Instead of the word theme though, I like to use a term I've stolen from screenwriters and that is *intent*. It took me almost ten years of writing and fifteen manuscripts to realize the critical importance of having an intent to my stories, beyond simply being entertaining, and having that intent in my conscious mind.

Someone in the screenwriting business once said you should be able to state your intent in three words. For example:

Love conquers all.
Honesty defeats greed.

There are others who say you need to be able to state it in one word:

Relationships.

Honesty.

Faith.

Fathers.

Think about what you want readers to *feel* when they've finished your book. You don't have to employ happy endings to leave your reader satisfied. You do, however, have to know what feeling you want the reader to experience and make sure you deliver. The more negative the intent, the better you have to be as a writer to keep the reader involved. To take readers on a dark and relatively unhappy journey, you have to be very good to keep them in the boat.

The more a reader *feels* about a book, the more he will get into it. Feeling comes out of the three aspects of a novel:

1. Idea.

2. Intent.

3. Characters.

If you know and, more importantly, have a good "feel" for each of these three before you begin writing, you increase the quality of your work. We'll talk about characters more in chapter six.

IDEA DOES NOT EQUAL STORY

There is a very big difference between the idea and the story. I've had great ideas that I couldn't transform into a story. On the other hand, I've taken some not so great ideas and pumped them up with a very good story.

The original idea is the foundation, the one-sentence beginning. Once you have the original idea, you have to figure out how you are going to tell that idea. That's the story. It's the building that goes on top of the foundation.

The difference between idea and story is one reason I'm not very nervous about sharing my ideas with others. I believe two people can have the exact same idea but they will come up with two very different stories.

An idea is usually an abstract. Many fledgling novelists start with the abstract, then got bogged down trying to get it on paper. That's why it's important to state your idea in one sentence and then write it down. Having it on paper makes your idea real. It makes the distance from idea to story less of a chasm. Even just thinking about your original idea is not good enough. You have to state it out loud and write it down on paper. Putting your thoughts on paper forces you to focus, and you might find that your great idea is actually difficult to state clearly.

It is a big jump from idea to story. Story includes characters, timing, point of view, pace, locale, etc. Story has to answer all the questions that come to mind the second you tell someone your idea. Story answers: Who? What? Where? When? How? It also answers the "Why" of your intent.

Watch the movie *The Player*. The writers try to pitch their concept to Tim Robbins's character. He says to all of them, "Tell it in twenty-five words or less." As a novelist pitching to agents or editors you get at most one paragraph to "hook" them and usually only one sentence. If you can't do it, you've got a problem with your idea.

On an episode of *Biography*, Clint Eastwood talked about his movies. For each, he'd say "The thing I liked about this screenplay was . . ." And he would sum it up in a sentence or two. He didn't go on and on saying, "Boy, I really liked the great scene on page twenty-eight and the twist on page forty-three and. . . ." Many writers get too caught up in the minutiae of their story and lose sight of the big picture. Eastwood bought the screenplay for *Unforgiven* based simply on this pitch: "It's the anti-Western." For someone like Eastwood, who made so many Westerns, the idea of doing the antithesis was intriguing.

What do you like about your proposed book? What will draw the reader in?

After you ask "what if?" of your idea, take it one step further. You will be surprised where it can take you. What if things aren't as they appear? As your writing gets more proficient, this technique will not only help you develop interesting plotlines, but it will also help you to add new layers to your story.

To further help yourself write your story, try talking it out with someone who knows nothing about it. If you can't succinctly explain it to another person, you are going to have difficulty writing it.

Keep in mind that almost everything has been done before. The secret is to do it somewhat differently. Many best-selling authors are writers who have "launched" a genre or who have taken it to new places. There was horror before Stephen King, but he took it to another level. He admits, for example, that *The Stand* was inspired by the idea of an earlier book, *Earth Abides*, but King took the idea to a higher level through the depth of his characters.

Do not write for the market. You don't know what the current trends are going to be in the two and a half to three years it will take you to get published. Instead, write what you feel you want to, and remember, if you want to sell it, you need to write it so other people will want to read it.

→TOOL: 4

YOUR PREPARATION

RESEARCH

Once you have figured out your original idea, and before you race off and start your story, you need to do research. When you're doing research, keep your mind open for all sorts of possibilities for your story. In fact, before you start writing the first word of your novel, go through the creative process outlined in this chapter, and make sure you know what you want to do before you trap yourself.

There are two types of research: primary and secondary. Both are important. Primary research is related to specifics of the story you are going to tell. Secondary research is ongoing and should be second nature to a writer (pun intended). You should constantly be observing things about the world. You should also be well read. Many times your ideas come out of a combination of primary and secondary research.

I had a demolition man on my Special Forces team, and whenever we went anywhere, he looked at things around him and thought about how he would blow them up. With every dam, power line, or bridge we passed, he estimated how many charges it would take and where he would place them. As a writer you should be thinking in similar ways. How would you write what you see and describe people that you observe? How would you show what you observe without telling?

As I've said before, the number one thing a writer must do is write. The number two thing a writer must do is read. Reading is a key part of research. Read for information and read for style. Read for format. Every book you read, you should be taking apart as I describe later in this chapter. When I get stalled writing, I'll turn around and look at the wall of bookcases behind me. I examine the titles of the books, remembering the stories. Looking at these books inspires me and, at times, provides me with ways around problems I'm facing in my current manuscript. Remember, as a writer, you are not alone if you have books.

You should also watch as many films as possible. Although the medium is different, the dramatic concept is basically the same.

In many cases, research helps you construct the story after you have your initial idea. Research doesn't just involve looking outward for information; it also involves looking inward. You have to develop your story line, locales, and characters. Also think about why your characters are acting a certain way. What do they think their motivation is and what is really their motivation? (We'll discuss this in the section about characters in chapter six.)

You can never have enough information. Even while writing, I look for more information about the topic I am writing about. All my books have started from the original idea, and then the story developed out of the research I did on that idea and related areas.

How factual should your story be? Where is the line between realistically portraying something and making things up? That's a difficult question to answer. My science fiction books are only science fiction in that I give a different explanation for things that actually exist. It is a fact that there are large statues on Easter Island. The fictional part of my book *Area 51* is when I give my own explanation for why those statues were made.

If you are writing a mystery, you can't be too far off base with your police procedural information. Many people are lulled by the inaccuracies portrayed in movies. Books have to be more accurate for several reasons: (1) Your average reader is more on the ball than the average movie goer; and (2) you can slide something by in a couple of seconds of film, but with a book, the reader can linger over and reread a paragraph. A reader can also turn back from page 320 to check page 45 where you mentioned the same thing and compare the two.

Earlier I mentioned many of the things you use for research. The Internet has become an extremely popular research tool. In addition to helping you gather information, the Internet also allows you to network. Nearly every possible organization out there has a Web site. There are numerous writers' organizations and writers' resource groups. You can even take a writing class on the Internet.

The Internet is also a useful way to get in contact with other writers and even agents and editors. I maintain a Web site of my own through which people can e-mail me.

Be warned though: You should spend the majority of the time on your computer writing, not surfing.

The Internet also can help you market your writing. I cover this in more detail in chapter nine, but a Web page is a valuable tool to promote your writing.

HOW RESEARCH CAN ADD TO YOUR STORY

Research helps begin the framework of story on top of the foundation of your original idea. For example, while I was writing *Area 51: The*

Sphinx, I was wading through a thick tome on the Great Sphinx, and one sentence in particular caught my attention. It said that Sir Richard Francis Burton, a man who'd always fascinated me, visited the Great Sphinx in 1855. The opening scene of the novel ended up being this very visit.

Research does more than just help you turn your ideas into story. It can also provide you with parts of the story, such as characters. Since one of my Atlantis books had half of its story line set in the year A.D. 1000, I was researching Vikings. I read about an interesting character named Corpse-Loddin, whose job involved sailing out in the spring to recover the bodies of Vikings who were trapped the previous winter by ice and killed. He would boil the bodies down, strap them to the side of his boat, and sail back home to sell the bodies to their families for proper burial. Corpse-Loddin seemed to be such a bizarre character that I knew he had to be in my story.

If you look in the acknowledgment sections of books, you will often find that the author thanks experts who helped with the research in the book. For a mystery this might include a police department, the forensics department, or the coroner. Undertaking such primary research for your own story can be very useful.

One problem to watch out for in talking with experts, though, is that they are usually more concerned with "getting it right" than with telling a story. As a novelist, telling a story is your priority. You have to listen carefully to the expert, shift through the mounds of information they are shoveling your way, and pick the nuggets of gold that you can use to make your story sparkle.

If you have to write about something you are unfamiliar with, "cheat." Find another fiction book that covers the same subject and see how that author wrote about a foreign topic. In fact, that's one of the reasons you need to read a lot and watch a lot of film—to add to your personal toolkit of techniques and information. Every now and then, you'll read or see something that really strikes you as being different. File it away in your mind to use in a later story.

For me, research is one of the "fun" parts of my job. Going to the library and looking through the stacks, checking magazines, videos, and the Internet is interesting. Keep your eyes open. Just because you are looking for a book filed under U410.L1 E38 doesn't mean you should ignore the books to the left and right of it. If you scan all the books that are shelved together you may come across a gold mine of information three books over from what you thought you needed.

BOOK DISSECTION

You've got your original idea, and you've done your research. Now, before you begin to write your book, you should find a published novel similar to what you plan to write. I guarantee you there is something out there that is similar. Once you find it, sit down with your razor sharp brain and cut it apart to see all the pieces. Then, put them together again to see how they all fit.

Ask yourself the following questions:

1. What was the original idea the author started with? How close is it to mine?
2. How did the author translate that idea into a story? What twist did the author put on the original idea? What's my twist? How is my idea different from this author's work?
3. What is the theme/intent to this story? What is mine?
4. Why did the author begin where he or she did? Where will I?
5. Why did the author choose the perspective he or she did? What will I choose?

6. What scope (bookends) did he or she place on the story? Bookends are beginning and end points for your story, usually thought of in terms of time—start point, end point, etc. What is mine?

7. What is the pacing of the story? How will I pace my story?

8. How did the author bring the story to a conclusion? How will I?

9. What did the author do that I liked? Can I do that?

10. What did the author do that I didn't like? Can I avoid that?

11. What didn't the author put in the book that I might have? Why didn't the author put that in?

12. What was in the book that I feel could have been left out? How would the story change if it were left out?

13. What were the subplots? How did they connect with the main plot? Did all the subplots get resolved?

14. Why did the author pick the settings he or she did?

I will address the topics of all these questions further in this book. You are going to face these topics in your own manuscript, and if you can understand how someone who successfully wrote the same type of book answered them, you can greatly improve your own ability to answer them. The more you read, the more the style and manner of the books you like will be imprinted in your conscious and subconscious brain, which will aid you greatly in writing your book.

Book dissection can also help you determine how "realistic" your book needs to be and how extensively you should research your topic. For example, in most mystery novels, police procedure lies somewhere between detective shows on TV and the way it is really done. If you interviewed a homicide detective about how she covers a murder scene, she would most likely give you great amounts of detail. If you incorporated all of her details into your scene, the resulting scene would have been many hours long and slow your action down. So see how such scenes are generally written in most novels that are published in your genre and proceed accordingly, no pun intended.

I have sat down with both best sellers and breakout novels, and dissected them on a spreadsheet, scene by scene, to study the structure. Many authors I've spoken with have done something similar in order to learn. You may want to take a book and give each scene in it a separate row on a spreadsheet, then in columns briefly describe the action, the characters involved, the point of view used, and the purpose of the scene, the last one being the most critical part. You can then study how a successful writer set up his own story.

After you dissect a book similar to the one you'd like to write, ask yourself, "How is my book going to be different? What is my unique twist?" Every idea has been done, so bring your originality to the development of your story from that idea.

TURNING IDEA INTO STORY

Given that you have now worked your way through deciding *what* to write, you face the second critical hurdle: deciding *how* to write it. Sometimes this hurdle can loom much higher than the "what" question. In fact, you may find that it causes you to reconsider your what. The transition from idea to story is not an easy one.

During this time, you must decide the who, what, where, when, how, and why of your story. There are an almost infinite number of ways to approach a story. This is also where the same idea can turn into two very different stories. Every idea has been done before, but every story hasn't been done before. Each one will be different.

When I was living in Korea, the power would be shut off, on average, once a day. No matter how often I remembered to save what I was working on, I would still lose some material. Ten minutes later, if I rewrote what I had just lost, it would be a little different than the original. I know there are days when I write something that if I had waited another day and written, the entire book would have turned out very differently.

In getting your original idea across to your audience, you have to decide upon the best mode and method. What perspective or point of view should you take? Where should the story start? How do you work in necessary background information? What subplots are needed to make the main story work? Can you tell your story that way and keep the reader interested? Can you pull off your surprise ending without cheating the reader? What sort of timeline should you use? How should the chapters be ordered? Should there be a prologue? An epilogue? All those questions and more eventually have to be answered when deciding how to translate your idea into a story that will span a novel. And you have to remember that all the answers interrelate and affect each other.

For example, let's say you have a magnificent idea for a novel spanning three centuries and multiple generations of a family on a farm in upstate New York. You plan to write about their trials and tribulations as they grow along with America. You feel so good about your idea that you are ready to sit down at the keyboard and start typing right away. But first there are a few questions you have to ask:

> **Where will you start?** With the first settlers in the family or back in the "old country" to show how and why the family ended up in America? Or will you start in the present and go backwards in time? How will you do the latter if you choose to go that way? Will you have someone find an old trunk in an attic full of papers, a diary, and photos? Why were they in the attic? Is the family moving and giving up the land? (That could add a special touch and urgency to the story.) Will you do parallel timelines? Jump back and forth? Will your reader

be able to follow your moving through time?

» **What will your perspective be?** Will you focus on every member of the family? The women? The children? Maybe you'll take the perspective of the land itself, which is one of the constants through the story. "But," you say, "how can I talk about the son who goes off to the Civil War?" If this son is killed, and his body brought back to be buried in the family plot, he becomes part of the land itself and he can tell his story, can't he? (See how every opportunity limits you only by the limit of you imagination?) Or perhaps you will tell the story of the family you want to highlight through the eyes of *another* family on the next farm.

» **How will you deal with the family secrets?** Keep in mind that not everyone in the family knows everything.

» **What is your intent?** What do your want readers to feel when they finish reading this story?

» **What is the climax of the story?** What is the story driving toward? How will everything come together?

» **Where will the story end?** Can you close out all your subplots with that ending? Does your ending offer readers enough of a payoff?

Do you see how many things you must think through before you start locking yourself in? The minute you write your first page, you have reduced a number of the possibilities of your technique and style. As a result, it's best to answer many of your style questions before you start writing in order to pick the one you feel best suits the story you want to tell.

Think of your novel as a cross-country race. You line your characters up at the starting line and fire the gun. You have a pretty good idea of where you want the finish line to be and a rough idea of the course, but things can happen along the way that will change the route. However, by the time all your characters get to the finish line, they will have to traverse the entire length of your story, page by page.

There are six important questions to ask yourself before you begin writing:

1. What do I want to write about?
2. What do I want to say about it?
3. Why do I want to say it?
4. Why should anybody else care?
5. What can I do to make them care?
6. What do I want readers to do, think, or see?

Most writers can answer the first three, but not the last three. The last three focus on the reader, while the first three focus on the writer.

Try to write like a reader, rather than a writer. That might sound strange, but as a writer, put yourself in the position of the reader. Ask the following questions: Have I hooked the reader? Am I maintaining suspense? What does the reader know up to this point? Remember, you're trying to get a story that's inside your head into the reader's head through the sole medium of the printed word. Try to constantly be aware of what you've developed in the reader's head.

The key to all the techniques and tools listed on the following pages is that they must be used to ensure *smoothness*. By smoothness, I mean that your writing must not jar the reader either in terms of style or story. The reader is interested in the story. Reading is the means by which she learns the story, but it is only a medium. The medium must not get in the way of the story. When the reader is pulled out of the story into the writing because you didn't use the proper technique, or didn't use it correctly, your writing is straying away from the story. A good maxim to keep in mind is: "Don't let them know you're writing."

VISUALIZING YOUR IDEA

I have mentioned the differences and similarities between writing and filmmaking. I do it to emphasize technique and also because we have a very visually oriented society. Every day, more people rent videos than check books out of the library. The filmmaking "camera" concept can help you, as the author, understand what you are portraying to the reader, especially in the area of perspective or point of view.

There are two concepts that are important to understand when trying to think like a novelist. First, you must be able to see a story with 360-degree vision (envisioning all possibilities), while simultaneously focusing in one direction well enough to be able to see over the horizon to where that particular possibility will lead. As an author, you must be able to see a multitude of possibilities in the story from the very first idea through the editing and rewriting stage. That wide range of vision allows you the ability to take the story in different directions that will make it more interesting and viable. Having blinders on severely handicaps your creativity. There are so many story possibilities inherent in every idea. You must see as many of those as possible and pick out the best one at each juncture.

Secondly, you must be able to see where each possibility leads with regards to your original idea, subplots, characters, timeline, etc. People usually have the mental capacity to work either way, but rarely can someone do both well. Some people see all the possibilities in every situation, but they cannot see the ultimate outcome of each possibility. Others can envision the ultimate outcome for a few possibilities, but they miss many of the other possibilities.

A successful writer must be able to do both. Since it can be difficult to do both well, you might want to consider discussing your work with a good friend who has a different perspective, or reading your work in a writers group for feedback. The problem with a novel is that it is very large, and a one-hour discussion is not going to cover all the areas you'd like to get feedback on. To get adequate help, you need someone who is not only good in the area you are lacking in, but also someone who is willing to put time and effort in to do a realistic and good job.

USING YOUR WRITING TOOLS

Very few novels in the bookstores were written in a vacuum. Certainly there are geniuses who have both talents and can do that, but for us mere mortals, we need help. And help should be an ongoing thing. To write four hundred pages and then give it to someone to read, only to have him say, "Hey, in chapter one, why didn't you do this?" can be quite frustrating. Remember your "camera" abilities when you think about writer's block. Quite often the "block" is the author trying to expand her mind to see other possibilities in the story, or trying to project out possible paths.

Warning: We are now moving into dangerous territory. We're going to be talking about theories, styles, and techniques. Most novice writers want formulas and rules. They want the answer that will make writing easy and get them published. Unfortunately writing is never easy and it takes much hard work to get published. Read the following words very carefully: There is no right or wrong way to write. There are only the right or wrong ways to use techniques and the right and wrong times and places to use techniques.

Does that make sense? In simpler terms, the words *never* and *always* should never be used when speaking of style (no pun intended). I emphasize the advantages and disadvantages of every writing technique in the following pages. You should do two things: Learn how and when to use the tool, and then know the advantages and disadvantages of each. Learning these two things will allow you to properly utilize the tools. It's like having a toolkit full of various implements. If you know how to use each one, and where and when to use them, you will be proficient in your craft. But none of the tools are *wrong*.

You can only use them improperly, or at the wrong time or place, or for the wrong job.

Carry that concept a little further: The more you understand the implements you have in your toolkit the better you can use them. The more I have written, the more I have come to understand the importance of knowing what I'm doing. That might sound a bit simplistic and naive, but in retrospect, I can quite honestly say I didn't really know consciously what I was doing when I wrote my first several manuscripts. I think the majority of my writing was based on the fact that I had read a lot. So when I chose my perspective, or my timeline, or developed my characters, I didn't do so consciously, but rather regurgitated the imprinted templates of all the novels I'd read.

Now, when I work on a manuscript, I may be doing the same thing I did on my first manuscript, but I am *aware* of what I am doing and this awareness allows me to improve my writing, opens up more story possibilities, and allows me to deepen my characters. I am able to wield my tools more effectively.

I liken this process to that of self-help books. I believe that self-help books only help a reader *after* he has already gone through the experience of change. Then the books serve two functions: (1) They confirm what the person has just learned; and (2) they explain what the person has learned. In this manner, it may be difficult to understand some of the tools or the way I have explained them if you have never written a manuscript. Study them anyway. Then, after you have written some, go back and reread these chapters. They will make much more sense in light of your writing experience.

As I mentioned, when I first started out, I didn't quite understand some of the things in writing books. I also smugly thought some of what was written in them was too "simplistic." Well, after many manuscripts, I am going back and saying, "Oh, yeah, *now* I get it. And, boy, this is a lot harder than it appears."

Furthermore, understanding the tools of writing may even allow a few of you truly innovative people out there to invent a new way to use an old tool. (Just be careful not to run with it in the wrong direction.) Your imagination is your only limit. There are ways around practically every limitation or disadvantage.

Before you start worrying about what tools or techniques to use, it is important for you to consider where you are going and what your objective is. For example, are you planning to self-publish your manuscript? Do you hope to find an agent? Are you going to use a book doctor? Know your goal and then evaluate everything in terms of that goal.

OUTLINING YOUR IDEA

At this point, you have completed the following in your creative process:

1. Stated your original idea in one sentence.

2. Researched everything that you can about your original idea.

3. Done a dissection on another book or movie that that used a similar original idea.

Now, it's time to translate your idea into story via an outline. I estimate I spend 25 percent of the time it takes me to complete a novel before I even write word one. Every day spent outlining and preparing saves me at least five days of actually writing.

When viewed in its entirety, a novel is very complex, particularly mainstream fiction. Working without an outline involves winging it. Every hour spent outlining prior to starting a novel saves you many hours in the actual writing process. Outlining also forces you to tighten down the story before you write, rather than having to do it during revision, which ultimately helps to produce a better work.

To be honest, the first time I fully outlined a novel was when I had a contract that called for a complete outline to be submitted to the publisher prior to final approval of the project (and, more importantly, a portion of the advance was to be paid on acceptance of the outline). Since then, I have found it to be a valuable tool. You are going to have to outline sooner or later when writing. You can do it as you go along or you can do it before you write. Doing it as you go along often causes you to waste a lot of time writing material that either has to be thrown out or extensively rewritten. It is prudent to do a lot of the thinking work ahead of time.

Another problem in working without a good outline is that you tend to get stuck about halfway through. When I first began writing this wasn't a major problem. My stories were basically straightforward action/adventure, and, while I didn't have a detailed outline, I did have a good idea of where I wanted the story to go. (They were based somewhat on personal experiences, which is, in essence, an outline.) I managed to blunder my way through. As I tried writing more complex stories, I found myself getting stuck more often and having to take days away from the keyboard to work out where the story was going and to keep the subplots in line.

When you start your manuscript with your one-sentence original idea, you have a relatively blank slate to work with. The further along you get, the fewer options you have. If you work without an outline, you may find yourself with *no* options at some point. Or at least no good options. This is, to slightly understate the predicament, not good.

The other chapters in this book present you with an overview of the pieces, such as narrative structure, the beginning, characters, etc., you need to put together a novel. Outlining puts those pieces into a framework. I cannot overemphasize (okay, I probably can) how important it is to have a feel for your characters before you begin writing. I consider getting that feel for your characters part of outlining.

Outlining is also critical in keeping your subplots subordinate to the main plot. You will restrict yourself from going off on tangents if you know at which point in your main story a subplot develops, and where and how it will eventually come back and tie into the main story line.

Here's another advantage to outlining: Since an outline is tight to start with, as you write and add flesh to it, you can make the story even tighter.

The degree of detail in your outline is personal. In fact, you may choose not to have one at all. But don't treat it like the gospel once you do devise one. As you go along, the story will develop a life of its own. As you fill in details, your story may even deviate from the outline. None of my recent, more complex novels turned out exactly the way I thought they would in the beginning, when all I had was the original idea and some research.

Also remember that outlining is an ongoing process, just as writing is. If you view a novel in the beginning as a large blank slate, then the original idea is a sentence you write at the top of the page. From there you start your outline, tracing characters and events along the timeline of your story. When you feel you have an adequate outline, you start writing. As the story progresses, you must go back every once in a while and redo the outline, tightening your story.

For instance, when you sense that you are losing track, review your outline and fill in what you've already written, adding all the details. Use the new details to redo the outline, tightening down what has yet to be written and making sure it is in congruence with what has already been written. Sometimes, you may have to go back and add a layer to the story, or even take a layer away. There are some critical questions that you must answer before you begin your manuscript. Answer these questions in writing, not in your head:

1. What is my one-sentence original idea?

2. Who are my main characters? What are their primary motivations? Do their primary motivations naturally lead them to assume the role they must, in this novel? How did they get these primary motivations? How do I *show* the reader the characters' primary motivations?

3. Where and when is my setting?

4. What is the climax of my story?

5. How do I maintain reader interest throughout the novel?

Caveat: Be careful that your writing doesn't appear to be just a blown up outline. When that happens, the writing will seem stilted and a little forced. Also, simply expanding an outline leaves little room for creativity and doesn't allow the characters to react and live. You may have outlined certain events occurring, but when you actually sit down and write your characters experiencing those events, will discover that it doesn't happen exactly as you outlined. Sort of like real life. Go with it. Allow your characters to be living beings involved in the story.

You'll have to find the degree of outlining that you are comfortable with, but do consider doing some sort of outline. There are some very successful authors who can break a novel down by sections, and structure and crank out certain genre novels according to a "script" they have for that type of book. And, although many don't like hearing it, there is a formula to some types of novels. Although we all want to be original (or maybe we don't?), realize that if you are writing a romance, and you produce something totally unlike any other romance on the bookshelves, you've done two things: (1) You haven't written a romance; and (2) when you try to market it, it won't be viewed as a romance. You may be a trailblazer and start a new genre, like those writers I mentioned earlier, but the odds aren't good. However, if you feel strongly about your writing, don't let the odds dissuade you, just be aware of the reality of the situation.

Every day when you sit down and start to write, you should update your outline. Pick a start point and an end point for every chapter. Then ask yourself: How do I get from one to the other? What is the purpose of this chapter? Also look at the chapter in terms of the overall story. Where does it fit? Is this the right time for this to happen? If you don't have a definite end point, your chapter will meander.

Appendix A is an example of a chapter outline that I used. While some of the story specific notes might not make sense to you, you can still get the gist of how a chapter outline can work. In a chapter outline, you should:

1. List the date and time at the top, putting it in time sequence for the story.
2. List the characters who will be in the chapter.
3. List the events in sequence, giving the major action and where it occurs.
4. Make notes on key material that must be dealt with later, in other chapters, or that already has been dealt with. This step is very important to ensure story continuity.
5. Have a definite start point at the beginning of the event sequence and a definite end point. List every important event that needs to occur in between.
6. Perhaps most importantly, give the purpose of the chapter. Where does the chapter fit within the overall story, and how does it move the story forward? How does it relate to the original idea? This will prevent your story from having extraneous material. Here are some examples of purposes for scenes and chapters (and the more of them you have in each scene or chapter, the tighter your book will be):

» Move the plot forward.

» Develop character and show character interaction.

» Explore setting, culture, values.

» Introduce new characters or subplot.

» Foreshadow climactic scene.

» Give expository information.

» Increase tension and suspense.

This is not to say that once you start writing the chapter, things won't change. But it is a heck of a lot easier to write with all the information thought out beforehand rather than making it up as you go. The outline allows you to concentrate on the writing since you know what you are going to put down.

The Catch-22 of Outlining. Not to contradict what I've written above, but there is a problem with trying to sit down and outline your very first manuscript. The problem is that since you've never written a manuscript, you are trying to outline something you've never done.

I have grown more fond of outlining the more I have written, but that is also a natural outgrowth of gaining more experience in novel structure and style. In knocking out my manuscripts, I've learned enough that I am able to outline quickly and effectively. I don't think I would have done anywhere as good a job on outlining my first manuscript. My recommendation on outlining is simple: Write down everything you think you know about your book. I say "think you know" because the transition from what you think are startlingly clear thoughts to paper can be very difficult. I've had great ideas that I thought would make great stories, but when I start actually sketching it out in the real world—on paper or on a computer—rather than in my head, I find things change considerably.

Because details drive the story, even with an outline, a story takes on a life of its own. No matter how detailed your outline, you can't think of everything. As you actually write the story, details will start popping up that will cause you to make changes. Most of the time these are details of reality.

For example, in your thriller you have a scene where your protagonist is searching out a series of tunnels, looking for the bad guys. The way you wrote your outline, the bad guy isn't in the tunnel and your secondary main character is sitting in her car above when she sees the bad guy escape. So she calls the protagonist on the radio, and he rushes to the surface for your climactic scene, right? Wrong. You can't use radio to get hold of someone underground. Or cell phones. This is a detail you might not have thought of when doing your outline but as you write it you realize it. So you change, you adjust. Just as details can limit you, they also provide give with different opportunities.

If you are following the flow of the sections of this book, they represent the way you might want to consider approaching your manuscript. By now, you've done a lot of legwork that you can put together to begin your outline.

→TOOL: 5

YOUR STORY

WHAT TO AVOID

Since I've spent a lot of time in my life looking at manuscripts, I keep a list of areas in which I see what I consider to be the most prominent problems. Initially, I focused on perspective as the major problem. As time went on though, and I learned more about the world of novels, I changed that opinion. If a manuscript's major problem is perspective, then at least the writer got out of the starting gate. Unfortunately, many writers never make it that far. I then decided that the lack of a strong original idea was the major problem with most manuscripts. Years after making that decision, I revised my list again. And again. And again. And after all those revisions, the point is this: Whatever the order of my list, mastering the elements on it—the elements of fiction—is key to successful writing.

The Beatles song "Paperback Writer" presents the writing profession as an easy road to fame and fortune. Anyone with access to paper and ink thinks he can join the ranks. However it is very important to learn the basic craft and elements of fiction before exercising one's genius. If you talk to coaches of teams, they always stress learning the fundamentals first—the same goes for writing. Too often, inexperienced writers jump deeply into too complicated a story before having the tools in order to set up the ability to make that leap.

In the following sections, I'll introduce you to the elements that can make or break your novel.

PERSPECTIVE/POINT OF VIEW

When a person has trouble writing action scenes, I immediately look to see if the author is handling perspective well. When dialogue drags, I check point of view. As a matter of fact, when there is any style problem, the first thing I look at is the point of view being used—the same way you would check the gas tank if a car's battery (the idea) was putting out juice, but the engine wouldn't fire.

Perspective is your voice as a writer.

CHARACTERS

A story can engage the reader on both the emotional and intellectual levels. The existence of strong characters can overcome a lot of style problems because the characters can touch the reader emotionally. When Anne Tyler wrote *Breathing Lessons*, the basic story involved two people driving from Baltimore to Pennsylvania for a funeral and then back home. Not the world's most startling idea or story. But the characters were portrayed so well, the book became a favorite of many, including me. I've learned that readers are more interested in people than anything else.

Gates of Fire, by Steven Pressfield, is about the battle of Thermopylae.

It's sold well. But what intrigues readers is not so much the battle, but the Spartans—readers are fascinated to learn how men could become soldiers who would stand and die to the last man in that mountain pass.

Why is Stephen King the number one horror writer? There are other writers out there who do horror as well as he does. But King writes great characters who draw the reader into the story, and when the horror strikes, it has more of an impact because of that emotional involvement.

If you want to see a great example of introducing characters and engaging readers with them, read the first ten pages of *Lonesome Dove*. Larry McMurtry, a master of multiple points of view, introduces Call, Gus, Newt, Jake Spoon, Deets, and several other characters in such a way that you immediately have a feel for them as real people.

THE IDEA

You've got to have a good idea. Too many manuscripts are written about events and characters that don't really interest any reader enough to get him to plunk down hard cash.

As I discussed in chapter three, it's vital to be able to state your idea succinctly. After you master that, find out if your idea works as a hook. Find a complete stranger on the bus on the way to work. Say to her, "I read a book the other day about [insert your idea]." How does she react? Is she interested? Does she call the police and have you carted off? Or, most likely, does she stare at you blankly without interest?

Your idea must intrigue your readers' intellect. Put good characters together with a great idea and the sky is the limit.

STORY

How many times have you picked up a book or heard about a movie that sounded interesting and then got turned off by the manner in which the story was told? A story can have an intriguing original idea and good characters, but the way the story is built upon those elements can make it a success or failure.

The story is a major stumbling block. I can pitch you ten good ideas at any moment. But it would take me a while to come up with a good supporting story for each of those ideas. In fact, for eight of the ten, I probably would not be able to come up with a good story at all.

I spend a lot of time working on story after I have an idea. I describe various stories to my friends, and we discuss them. Ultimately, and you are going to cringe to hear this, I don't proceed with a story line until it *feels* right. This is part of the artistic craft in writing, and a pretty realistic one. You have to feel comfortable that you can write your story and that it is interesting not only to you, the writer, but also to the reader.

TIMELINE OR PACING

Timing can be a big problem in manuscripts because too many writers don't knock the reader's socks off with their opening two chapters. Yet, most of us aren't good enough writers to spend a hundred pages drawing the reader in. You have to hook them and hook them fast.

At the same time, it's important not to rush through your story. Write scenes, not incidents. Make sure you tell the story, instead of just relaying information to the reader. Try to write a scene in "real time" from beginning to end, rather than jumping around or using the fast forward button. (You'll find more information on how to start and end your novel later in this chapter.)

In addition to the above elements, I constantly find more specific problems in manuscripts, too. (You'll find more information on them in the various sections that follow.)

1. Hooking the reader. Many writers spend too much time giving background information, introducing various characters, etc., before they introduce: (1) the plot; and (2) the main character.

2. **Dialogue tags.** The words inside the quotation marks have to get across to the reader the necessary information and emotion. Trying to make up for the lack in written dialogue by overusing dialogue tags is a common and very jarring problem.

3. **Repetition.** Using the same words or phrases over and over can distract the reader.

4. **Time sense or the "remote control effect."** A story should flow in some sort of logical time sequence. Too often stories fast-forward, then rewind to a flashback, jump forward again, slow down, speed up, etc., until the reader's head is spinning.

5. **Setting the scene.** Often I begin reading a scene or chapter and am totally lost for several pages as to where this action is occurring, who is in the scene, and when this scene occurs in relation to the last scene.

6. **Characters talking to themselves.** This is a weak technique to give expository information or thoughts to the reader. What do you think of someone who wanders around talking to herself all the time? Also, this technique used in conjunction with an actual conversation can be very confusing because the reader will not be sure which dialogue is directed at the other participant in the conversation and which is directed back at the speaker.

7. **Misuse of pronouns.** If you have two men in the room and use the phrase, " 'Blah, blah, blah,' he said," it had better be very clear which "he" you are referring to. Be very clear about whom your pronoun refers to. Don't confuse the reader.

8. **The difference between a memory and a flashback.** Basically, memory is what someone remembers happening, tainted by subsequent events and the person's emotions; a flashback is what actually happened.

9. Slipping into second-person point of view. Any time you address the reader as I am now addressing you, you are using second-person point of view. This becomes a problem when it causes a jarring shift from the point of view of the rest of the book.

NARRATIVE STRUCTURE

If you'd like a blueprint for a novel then I give you the five elements of narrative structure:

AN INCITING INCIDENT

The inciting incident constitutes the hook. It's a dynamic event and should be seen as such by the reader. The incident should upset the balance of forces, and the rest of your novel should be an attempt by your protagonist to restore the balance.

A good way to twist the inciting incident is to have what appears to be a positive event turn out to be the worst thing that could possibly happen to the protagonist. Think of the stories you've heard of someone winning the lottery and it ruining his life.

A SERIES OF PROGRESSIVE COMPLICATIONS

Progressive complications escalate the conflict. Suspense is an integral part of practically any story, whether it involves a hero saving the world or the inner transformation of a main character. There are many types of suspense.

Consider, for example, the movie *Dancer, Texas Pop. 81*. The movie chronicles a weekend in a small Texas town. It starts on Friday, with a high school graduation of a class of five (four boys and one girl) and follows the four boys over the weekend through Monday morning. When they were sophomores, the four bought bus tickets for the Monday morning after graduation so they could get the heck out their small town and go to Los Angeles. The suspense comes from wondering which of the four will be on that bus Monday morning and which will stay. Since you come to care about these characters, you care about the decisions they will make. As Monday approaches, the level of suspense rises.

Suspense in a thriller can come from a clock ticking. In a mystery it can arise from the classic "who-done-it." Many mystery manuscripts I see lack suspense—if it is a one-time murder, how are you going to generate suspense? Sometimes it's from *how* the good guy catches the bad guy. But if you just have a body, and there's no threat that the killer will kill again, or that the hero is in danger, or there isn't a hint of some payoff, then there's little suspense.

Many writers believe suspense comes from having a surprise near the end of the novel. The problem with this method is that the reader doesn't know the surprise is coming, so therefore there is no suspense. Even if you have a surprise ending, you still must escalate conflict to keep the suspense level rising until the reader gets to the surprise.

A CRISIS

Another element of narrative structure is the crisis. At the point of crisis, the protagonist is forced to make a choice whether or not she wants to attempt to restore the balance that was disrupted by the inciting incident. It should not be obvious to the reader how the crisis is going to be resolved. You raise suspense by keeping the reader guessing. The crisis is usually the darkest moment for the protagonist.

CLIMAX

With a climax, the choice is made, and balance is either restored or a new balance is worked out. Make sure your protagonist is involved in the climax. The climactic scene is your protagonist and antagonist bringing the problem introduced at the beginning of the book to a conclusion.

RESOLUTION

Wrap up your plots and subplots; don't leave any loose ends dangling. The reader cares about all the characters and all the events. Tie it all up. Most of the time, the resolution provides the reader with a sense of closure by highlighting the emotional payoff the reader gets from the entire book.

I present the narrative structure as a guideline for those who wish to use it. There are certainly novels that don't follow it, and some genres, such as thrillers, mysteries, science fiction, and fantasies, fit into this structure much more clearly than others do. Examine the narrative structure when breaking down the novel you dissected earlier.

You can also use narrative structure when approaching the question of story. Your idea might be the hook, or it might be the crisis,

INTRODUCING THE PROBLEM

If a novel has a problem that needs to be resolved, who usually introduces the problem? The antagonist. Taking the point of view of the antagonist during outlining can help you focus the plot of the novel. Your protagonist will be reacting to the antagonist's plan until the critical moment at which the protagonist starts to act.

Before I start a thriller, I spend a considerable amount of time figuring out the antagonist's goals and plans. The antagonist's motivation must be believable to the reader and the plan must be viable.

or it might be the decision that is made. The question is, can you create a complete story that has a resolution?

PLOT

When I looked up the definition for plot in a dictionary, it said: A secret plan to achieve a hostile or illegal purpose. Just joking. A more applicable definition is: The series of events consisting of an outline of the action of a narrative or drama.

Notice the definition says a "series of events." That means something has to happen. Most of us can't get away with writing a story where your characters stand around doing nothing. Action, in whatever form it takes, moves the story forward and carries the characters with it. Sometimes your characters act, sometimes they react. Regardless, they're doing something.

Try to have an idea of what the climax of your story will be before you've even written the first sentence. After all, that's what all the action is driving toward. Knowing the climax before you start writing will help give your story direction and keep you focused on the main plot. It also prevents you from getting sidetracked and making a subplot develop into the climax of the book. Without an idea of what the climax is, you might end up with a book that will never end.

Time is linear and moves forward. The same is usually true with plot. Flashbacks and memories can be dangerous because they reverse the time flow. That's not to say it's wrong to use them, but be aware what they do to the time flow of your story.

Real life is full of coincidences, but there is great debate over how much coincidence can or should come into play in a novel. Some people say you should have no coincidences at all in a book, that everything must happen for a reason. The thinking behind that is to prevent the author from manipulating the plot too much. But, the author is, after all, the supreme ruler of the novel, so in essence the entire novel is a manipulation.

Others feel that coincidence can drive a novel. In an article titled "Nine Precepts for Writing a Popular Novel," author Bryce Courtenay describes the "power of coincidence" as, "the unlikely premise that you might not accept in real life but which turns out to be a fascinating and complex resolution over the length and breadth of your novel." He advises writers not to ignore coincidence, as "most of us are superstitious by nature and superstition is essentially built on coincidence."

When does a coincidence work? When it is an integral part of the novel. In Michael Connelly's novel *Blood Work*, a retired FBI agent is asked to investigate a murder by a relative of the victim. The agent is recovering from a heart transplant operation and doesn't want to take the job on, until he finds out that the heart he received came from the victim. A staggering coincidence, right? Not when you find out that someone murdered several people in an attempt to get a different type of transplant. Thus the "coincidence" turns out to be a plan by someone and, as a result, drives the entire story and provides the climax.

When doesn't such a coincidence work? When it comes outside of the plot to change the plot. Example: Your hero is trying to find out who the bad guys are. The phone rings, and the secretary for one of the bad guys gives your hero the much needed information. This is the first time this character has appeared, and afterward, we never hear from or see the secretary again; she was an obvious plot device to jump-start the novel and dump information. (The phone call works, however, if it's an attempt by the bad guys to lure the good guy into an ambush.)

When working out your plot, keep the term *internal logic* in mind. A plot needs to make sense inside of itself.

SHOW, DON'T TELL

If you've ever attended a writing class or conference, this phrase has fallen upon your ears again and again. What exactly does it mean?

First, let me say that it isn't completely true all the time. There are indeed times in a novel when you should tell. In fact, telling is one of the advantages a novelist has over a screenwriter who must stay completely in the showing mode.

Also, the line between showing and telling is nonexistent at times. It's a sliding scale. At one end (telling) is pure exposition; at the other end (showing) is dramatization. Telling tends to summarize information, giving it secondhand. Showing allows you to see, hear, feel, smell, and taste firsthand.

Some things to keep in mind when considering whether to show or tell:

1. **Don't do information dumps.** Too often people lead with information rather than plot. Information should only be given to the reader when it is absolutely necessary *at that moment* for the reader to understand the plot. Too many writers give information too soon, and the reader doesn't know why he is being given this material.

   Also, many people open a book with a nice opening line or paragraph and then suddenly go into memory or flashback. If you have a memory or flashback in your opening chapter, perhaps you are starting the book in the wrong place.

2. **Match showing and telling to the inherent pace of your story.** If you have a fast-moving thriller, a lot of telling can really slow the story. On the other hand, if you are writing a multigenerational family saga, there will probably be a lot of telling. Learn to mix the two.

3. **Try to always show action.** Don't have your action occur offstage. Summarized action is boring.

4. **Always show the climax of the book.** And have your protagonist and antagonist in the scene. It's also a let down to the reader—and a weak climax—if your two main characters are present in the climactic scene.

As with all the other elements of the book, creating a successful plot involves learning the craft and then using it as you see fit as an artist.

STARTING YOUR NOVEL

There are actually two beginnings to a novel: the first words the writer puts down to start the manuscript, and the first words the reader sees as she opens the completed book. These two sets of words are not always the same. When I teach novel writing, I find most students spend an inordinate amount of time trying to have the perfect beginning, but since writers often rewrite their work extensively, much of that time is wasted. My advice is to just start somewhere and sometime. You can always go back and redo the beginning. The number one rule in novel writing is simply, *write*.

Now that we've cleared that hurdle, let's discuss the beginning of a novel in conceptual terms. Understanding the diagram below will help us in doing that:

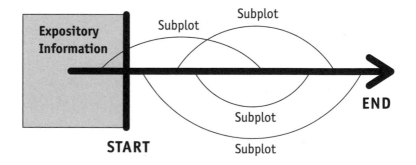

Let me explain what each part represents:

The thick vertical line on the left, labeled "Start," is where the novel begins. Page 1.

The tip of the arrow on the right, labeled "End," is where the novel ends. Last page.

The thick horizontal arrow, going straight across, is your original idea or the main story line.

The thin lines are your subplots and ancillary action. Note that all subplots eventually end up supporting the original idea and close out before the end of the novel.

The shaded box before the start point is known as your expository information, or more simply, the background or the backstory. There is always a history prior to the start point of the novel—a history of the characters, the locale, the environment, the crisis to be faced—the list goes on and on.

WHERE TO BEGIN AND WHAT TO INCLUDE

When trying to decide where to place the start line, keep in mind the purposes of the beginning of a book. Your opening chapter has to bring people in the door. The beginning must hook the readers and also either introduce the story theme or problem, or introduce the main characters. It could do both, but don't overwhelm your reader by putting too much in the first chapter.

By knowing all the information in your expository information box, you give yourself the ability to dip into that box and write a new beginning, sliding the start line to the left. If you slide the start line to the right, you simply have to expand your expository information box by removing the information you originally had in your beginning and working it in later in the story.

In the movie *Memento*, the story begins at the end and progresses back in time. The writer, Christopher Nolan, presents the resolution of the crisis and then proceeds to show how that resolution comes about and what starts the crisis in the first place. I wonder if the writer originally wrote it that way, or if he scripted it in normal time sequence and then reversed the whole story. The finished product, in essence, reverses the story line. Keep this in mind while starting your own writing. When you're starting your book, most likely you won't be able to decide the correct place to put your starting line until you have drawn out that original idea to its conclusion. You can always go back and adjust the start point.

By the end of your second chapter, you should have: (1) introduced the core problem that will be resolved in the climax; and (2) introduced your protagonist (if you haven't already). Think about the message you send with your opening. If you lead with your problem, you are telegraphing to your reader that the problem is key. If you lead with your main character, then you are telling the reader the character is more important.

Start noticing how books and movies start. Figure out why the writer started them the way he did. There is a reason. To check to see if you have an exciting opening, sit back, close your eyes, and visualize your opening as if it were a movie. Is it exciting? Enticing? Boring?

When starting your story, remember that you have to hook the reader very quickly within a few pages. Hopefully within the first sentence. Some writers spend too much of the beginning giving background information that sets up a hook. You don't have that luxury. Go to the bookstore, take books off the shelf, and read the opening paragraphs or lines. You'll start seeing a common thread, where the authors try to quickly evoke a mood to get you interested in the story. Do your best to engage a reader's intellect and his emotions as quickly as you can.

Some writers make the mistake of hiding their story. This is what author John Saul calls a "secret-keeper." If the reader can't find the story quickly, then all the expository information, the setting, the characters—everything the reader receives—will be confusing since she doesn't have the framework of story to place all the information upon.

INCLUDING THE BACKSTORY

Depending on the type of novel you are writing, the expository information box can be very small or very large. For example, a science fiction writer setting a story in the twenty-fourth century has a very big box that he has to understand and develop before he can even begin to write the start.

Notice that the beginning of the arrow of the original idea, and many of the subplots, begins prior to the start point of the novel. This means to you, the writer, two things. First, *you* must know all the information in this box prior to beginning your writing. You must know about your characters and all the background information necessary to make a believable story. Failing to do this essential background work sabotages the story before you type your first word—your lack of preparation will become very apparent to readers as they progress through your novel.

Secondly, it means there is usually vital information the *reader* must eventually have about things that existed and events that occurred prior to the book's start point in order to comprehend what she is reading. How you relay this information to the reader is extremely important. Naturally, it must be worked in smoothly. Work in the background information the reader needs in glimpses, when it's required to understand the present story. In most cases, try not to use whole chapters to do this as it slows down your story. A common mistake beginners make is to write an excellent opening chapter presenting the crisis or hook, and then have three chapters of necessary background material to fill in all the background the reader needs to know. Once you initiate action, you shouldn't pause it for backstory— keep the story going.

Slip in background when needed and when it answers questions the reader will have. Provide background information when the normal reader would get to a certain part of your narrative and start picking up his hand to scratch his head because he needs to know something he doesn't. Give him the information before the hand reaches the head.

Try to use dialogue or authorial narrative (omniscient point of view) to present that information; this is preferred over simply having characters thinking and remembering because then you don't have to constantly filter the information through your character's thoughts and senses. You can also use flashbacks, but use them correctly. You must have a good lead into the flashback and a smooth lead back into the action of the narrative. Flashbacks work when you smoothly integrate them, and when you place them at the point where the reader is interested in finding out the background information you are going to present.

Also, remember there is a difference between a flashback and a memory. A memory is a character's viewpoint on a past event. A memory can give the event more relevance to the current story but can also warp the reality of what really happened.

You must not only slide in and out of flashbacks smoothly in the story line, but you must also do it smoothly style-wise. The first and last paragraphs of the flashback should move out of and back into the paragraphs on either side of the flashback. For example, you are writing about a man sitting at his desk at work, getting ready to make a life-changing phone call. You move into a flashback giving necessary information as to why the phone call has to be made by starting the flashback with *another* phone call in the past. Then you can move back to the present with the phone in the present ringing, bringing both character and reader back to the present. A simple and obvious ploy, but better than just plunking down the flashback in the middle of your chapter and confusing the reader as to the timeline.

WHEN TO START

Another aspect to consider when deciding where to start your novel is its timeline. This decision can greatly affect your writing and style.

There are many ways to arrange the timeline of the story, but the most important thing to remember is to keep the reader clued in. It is extremely confusing to the reader if his sense of time in the story gets screwed up.

Let me give you an example of timeline problems: I recently reviewed a manuscript telling the story of two brothers during the Civil War. The author had to pick a start point and then move his story forward from there. At first he picked Appomattox. However, after that, he constantly went back to battles during the war, such as the first and second battles of Bull Run and Antietam. The shift in style required to make these moves was jarring to me as a reader.

The author then rewrote the story starting at the second battle of Bull Run. The only problem he now had though, was in style. Once you lock into a time frame for the story with a start point, you must make sure your tenses indicate to the reader whether she is in the normal time frame of the story, or moving back in time prior to the start point. The reader assumes that you are going to progress in a sequential fashion. You don't necessarily have to, but you must remember to take her along with you when you do make your shifts. Read and study other writers' styles to see how they achieve these shifts. Another problem this writer had with his original starting point was that he lost all his suspense during his chapters that went back into the war because we already knew who was alive at the end of the war . . . and who won the war.

Some writers start their books with a prologue, others with chapter one. What's the difference? A prologue is used when the material you want to include in the opening is out of time sequence with the rest of the story.

PACING YOUR NOVEL

While the beginning of your novel can be fun to write and the end is most certainly exciting, the bulk of the novel lies between. Wherever you decide you want to start, you must get to the end in a manner that doesn't lose or confuse the reader. What you want to avoid is the remote control effect I referred to earlier. A novel should employ a smooth pace, but many writers jerk the pace around by pausing, and using slow motion and fast-forward. They speed up when they're writing a scene; they spend too much time on scenes they enjoy. The finished product ends up jerking both the pace and the reader around. To avoid an uneven pace, you need to examine the pace of your story overall and by chapter.

OVERALL PACE

The reader will quickly grow to expect a certain time sequence and pacing in the book. Remember the number one rule of writing is to not jar the reader.

In published books, you can find pretty much every possible time sequence. You can read books that go forward in time every fifty years, those that bounce back and forth between the present and the past, and those that go into the past, present, future. Those that use parallel time sequences. You name it, it's been done and you can do it. But remember the poor reader. Make sure he can follow what you're doing. When first starting out, I recommend trying to use normal time sequence as much as possible simply because it is easier.

When thinking about the pace for your entire novel, think about chapter length. It may be helpful to envision a chapter to be a set length of time in the story. Use chapter breaks when there is a change, usually in time, point of view, or setting. Sometimes, writers may end one chapter and start the next with the same point of view, time, setting, and characters. This technique can be used to make a point.

You also may want to consider "bookends" for your story—a time or geographical framework in which to put your story line. Bookends will help you focus your story line by providing set starting and stopping points. For example, James Grady's *Six Days of the Condor* employs time bookends: It takes place in six days. (Although the popular film version, *Three Days of the Condor*, altered that time frame.)

PACE WITHIN A CHAPTER

I just looked at a sample chapter that featured an opening paragraph with the main character packing up to leave her home; in the second paragraph the character was in a new town; in the third she was in a job interview for a new job, a part that went into much more detail and extended for several paragraphs; then another paragraph jumped weeks ahead. There are two major problems with this approach. First, it is disconcerting for the reader to not know where she is both time and location-wise every time she starts a new paragraph, never mind a chapter. Second, the writer covers a major event, such as a move in one paragraph, and then several paragraphs later uses the same amount of words for describing an office. In the mind of the reader, it makes these two events equal in significance because of the amount of writing given to both, even though they obviously aren't. If you spend two paragraphs on A and two paragraphs on B, the reader will think A equals B. They might not seem equal to you, but you always have to consider what the reader thinks.

Such jerking around is a classic example of remote control effect at work on the paragraph level. Beware of time sequence changes on the chapter level—use them poorly, and you risk losing your reader. An analogy: You can either watch a video in real time or you can use the fast-forward. But every time you use the fast-forward or the slow motion, you lose something. Keep it steady.

Of course, you say, can't a time sequence change catch the reader's attention and be used in a positive manner? Of course. Just make sure you understand that there *is* a pace to a story and do it consciously.

A chapter is a specific chunk of time. Try to write a scene from beginning to end inside a chapter. If additional events in different places with different characters are happening at the same time, skip a few lines and write these additional scenes in the same chapter to indicate they're occurring at roughly the same time.

One method used to get the reader oriented to the pace is to use headers. You can open every chapter, and introduce locales within the chapter, with a header like:

West Point, New York

14 November 1997

10:23 A.M. local/ 1523 Zulu

Quite honestly, while a valid technique, using headers is also a bit of a lazy one. At times, I've employed headers with stories that shifted so quickly to so many locations, across numerous time zones, that I felt they were needed to keep the reader oriented.

It is important to keep in mind, however, that readers often don't read headers. If you must use one, still try to back it up in the first paragraph by letting readers know where they are, what time it is, and what characters are present.

If you don't use headers—and odds are you won't—you really must make sure you orient your reader quickly, usually in the first paragraph. If readers spend too much time wondering about locale, time, and characters, they will start losing interest in the story.

If you are writing suspense, there is usually a "clock ticking" in the story. A deadline approaching adds suspense to a story and gives your story a definite timeline. If you're writing suspense, try not to initiate the ticking too quickly, because doing so makes it more difficult to develop your characters adequately. You can introduce the problem the story revolves around in the first two chapters, but then you probably need a couple of chapters letting the readers get to know your characters well before you thrust them all into the maelstrom of the plot.

ENDING YOUR NOVEL

The end is the resolution of the problem that you introduced in one of the first two chapters. But remember all that expository information you worked in along the way? You must also close out all your subplots by the end, which sometimes can be quite difficult to do.

Study endings as much as you study beginnings. Why did the author use an epilogue? How did he explain all the hidden details that bring the conclusion together? How many chapters did the author write after the climactic scene?

The end line on the diagram from page 80 is not as flexible as the beginning line. When the end comes in your story, it comes. Because you have all those prior pages, you lose some degree of control over your ending. It should be a *natural* conclusion of the story.

As I discussed earlier, it can be helpful if you have an idea what the climax of your book is going to be before you start writing it, as that is what the story is driving toward. Some writers don't want to do that—you have to find what works for you.

We have all read books where the endings rang flat or disappointed us. The question you should ask yourself as a writer is, "Why did that ending disappoint?" A book should have a payoff for the reader.

If you don't have a good idea of your ending when you start writing, your story may tend to wander. If your plot is complex and you don't have an idea for your ending, you might not come up with a strong ending at all, as everything simply unravels and you can't tie together all the loose threads to end the book succinctly and in a satisfactory manner.

It all goes back to outlining and whatever you feel comfortable with. The most important thing about the ending is to close out your main story line and all your subplots. Don't leave the reader guessing.

Also note that in the narrative structure, the climax is not the same as the resolution. The climax ends the crisis. The resolution explains how the crisis is over and also lays out the effect on the characters who must now go on. In Stephen King's *The Stand*, the climax is the defeat of the Walking Man. The resolution is what happens in Boulder when the survivors return.

HOW LONG SHOULD A MANUSCRIPT BE?

This is a frequently asked question and one that is dangerous to answer. The standard answer is: as long as the quality of writing can support.

If you have to haul your manuscript in to an editor's office in a wheelbarrow, you might get an initial negative impression, but if the quality of the writing and story makes it a magnificent opus, then he'll buy it.

On the other end of the spectrum, *The Bridges of Madison County* was perhaps 50,000 words.

Generally, though, the normal manuscript length is between 75,000 and 100,000 words. Most of mine seem to be around 100,000 words or 400 manuscript pages. My longest was 580 manuscript pages and my shortest just over 300.

The manuscript has to be long enough to tell the story well.

→TOOL: 6

YOUR TECHNIQUE

CHARACTERS

You've probably heard it said that there are two ways to write a book. The first is to come up with a plot and then find characters to live the story. The second is to come up with characters and then write their story. I say do both. Remember one thing though—it will be people who read your book, and people identify primarily with people, not plots or facts. Another thing to consider is that many times your characters *are* your plot. By this, I mean that once your characters come alive, they, not you, direct where the story will go through the choices they make.

Regardless, you need people in your story. Or maybe aliens. Or an interesting rabbit such as Richard Adams in *Watership Down*. Or perhaps a wisteria vine as in Clyde Edgerton's *Floatplane Notebooks*. You need characters, even if they are inanimate.

In the army we used to get asked which came first: the mission or the men? The approved solution was the mission (read plot). My answer was always the men (read characters) because without the men you can't accomplish the mission. In the same manner, you need good characters regardless of the story, and if you keep them "in character" they will dictate what is going to happen in your story.

Appreciating the importance—indeed the preeminence—of characters in a novel is a three-stage process. First, you have to accept that characters are the most important aspect of the story. Of course, it is possible to create a manuscript that is so character oriented there is little to no plot. The second step is to spend as much time developing your characters *before* starting the novel as you spend outlining your plot. Some people might be able to invent plot or characters on the fly as they write, but I find the time spent before starting, is time well invested.

The third, and most difficult step, is to figure out how to *show* who the characters are, instead of simply telling. What actions, dialogue, and decisions will show the reader the nature of the characters, even as the characters themselves remain unaware of some of the aspects of their own personalities?

Ask yourself, "Who are my characters? Do I have a good feel for who each person is?" If you don't, you will find that your characters are two-dimensional and inconsistent. Your characters must be as true to you as people you know in the real world.

What do your characters look like? You may know, but you will be surprised how many times characters are never really described to the reader. I felt very stupid after someone read my 450-page manuscript only to ask, "Very interesting, but what did your main character look like?"

It is important to describe characters as early in your novel as possible. If you don't, the reader will formulate his own vision of the character, and then you may jar him three chapters down the line when you finally get around to describing the character and it doesn't fit the reader's mental vision. Try to describe characters in such a way that something about each one will stick in the reader's mind. This technique is especially important the greater the number of characters you have.

Sometimes, authors choose not to describe their characters because they want readers to think of "every man" or "every woman" when they think of each character. That's fine as long as there is a purpose to it.

NAMING YOUR CHARACTERS

Character names are very important. You have to decide if you are going to use a character's first name, last name, title (e.g., the doctor, the captain, etc.), or nickname. Your character's name should give you a feel for what kind of person she is.

How do you pick names for your characters? The phone book is helpful. Go to the library and wander the stacks and look at author names. Check high school and college yearbooks.

You do need to consider that the name fits the character. Many names denote ethnicity. Think about detectives—don't they all have hard sounding names like Magnum P.I.? Such names are deliberately chosen to affect you subconsciously.

Make sure two characters don't have similar names. Try to avoid even having names that start with the same letter.

Stick with one name for each character. If you use a character's nickname, formal name, and job title, all the various names can confuse the reader. If you alternate between using first and last names for your characters, you are doubling the number of names the reader has to remember. Pick one name and stick with it as much as possible. Of course there will be times when other names and titles come into play, such as in dialogue, but in your prose, make it as easy on the reader as you can.

BUILDING YOUR CHARACTER'S PERSONALITY

So what else do you need to know about a character? First, you need to know her motivation, why she acts the way she does, and what she desires. You should also consider the following questions:

1. What does your character look like? How does she talk? How does she act physically? Any mannerisms?
2. What is her background? Where was she born? What were her parents like? How was she raised? Where did she go to school? What level of education?
3. What is her job? What special skills does her job require, and how will they affect her role in the story? What are her hobbies and talents?
4. Who's in her family? Does she have a husband? How is her relationship with him? Does she have children? If not, why not? Is she divorced? Why? Why not?
5. Where is she from? Did she grow up in a city or on a farm?

Some other aspects of a character to keep in mind:

> » Dress.
> » Attitudes.
> » Gestures.
> » Manner.
> » Culture.
> » Social class.
> » Values and beliefs.
> » Needs.
> » Dreams.
> » Fears.
> » Stressors.

I highly recommend putting some thought into your characters before writing your first page as opposed to making them up as you go along. I say this from my own experience. *The New York Times* review of my second novel, *Eyes of the Hammer*, said, "The characters are right out of Action Comics." Not very nice, but true. I learned my lesson.

Now, here's something to consider: You can make up your characters by using the list of questions mentioned earlier. But, reality says that you will create more realistic characters by using people you have met, like your mother and father and the loan officer at the bank. Look at the people you know as character *types*, and use some of their traits.

You can also try psychology. There are several books on the market that have tests that will define people by type. Use these books to help round out your characters. Once such test is the Myers-Briggs Test, found in *Please Understand Me: Character and Temperament Types* by David Keirsey and Marilyn Bates. The test divides people into sixteen personality types, and lists the good and bad tendencies of each type, which you can use to develop well-rounded characters. The typical interactions between the various personality types are also listed.

YOUR CHARACTERS' ACTIONS

You make believable characters by showing how they act and react in a crisis. Actions speak louder than words. Also remember, though, that the same action done for two different reasons makes the action seem very different to the reader. Your main character kills someone. Is that bad? It depends, you say, on who she killed, why she killed him, and under what circumstances.

Remember all those questions, because eventually you will have to answer every one of them for the reader. They also give you the opportunity to put some twists in your story. For example, character C kills character J in chapter three, making C look like a bad egg. But in chapter seven, you reveal that the deceased, J, was in reality a mad scientist about to let loose a plague upon the world, and C stopped that by killing him. That certainly changes the reader's perspective on C.

You say a lot about your characters by showing what choices they make under pressure. Sometimes a person's personality totally changes when she is under stress, and the "real" person comes out. Such a change can be useful in your plot and story line. A character can appear to be one type of person, but in a crisis, become someone else entirely.

Even if it won't appear in the book, know your characters' backstory. Writing it out will help you write believable characters. All of your characters have a background prior to the beginning of the novel. Make sure you know it and, where applicable, let the reader know parts of it in order understand the characters better.

Now, the astute reader is saying: "Hey, you're contradicting yourself. Earlier you said to let a character's actions speak for themselves. How am I going to reveal motive only by action, without getting into my character's thoughts?"

My question to you is: How do you know anyone's thoughts other than your own? Through conversation, and through watching their actions over a period of time and interpreting them. All through various means and all short of saying "Jim thought. . . ."

Taking it a step further, if you are always in your characters' heads, how can you keep a motive secret, something that might be essential to the suspense of your story? I'll give you ways to do this when I explain point of view later in this chapter.

CHARACTERS AND CONFLICT

Conflict keeps a story going and reveals much about your characters. Conflict is the gap between expectation and the actual result. There are three levels of conflict for your characters:

» Inner conflict (inside the character).

» Personal conflict (between characters).

» Universal/societal conflict (characters versus fate/God/the system).

You have to consider what your main character faces on each of these levels. There are five major sources of conflict for people (although you can probably come up with more):

» Money.

» Sex.

» Family.

» Religion.

» Politics.

Keep these sources of conflict in mind when developing your characters.

Remember all characters have to have an agenda or goals they want to achieve. That gives them a driving force, even if it is a passive or negative one. Characters can pursue their goals aggressively or subtly. Or they can not pursue their goals, which also says something about them.

CHARACTERS AND MOTIVATION

Motivation is the most important factor to consider when having your character make choices. For your characters to be realistic, they have to react like the people you have developed them to be, not like you want them to react in order to move your story ahead. Every time a character acts or reacts, ask yourself if that is consistent with whom you projected the character to be.

For example, in my novel *Atlantis*, I wrote a scene in which some people were trying to talk my main character into traveling back to Cambodia where he had last been more than thirty years ago. It was also the site where his Special Forces team had been wiped out in a horrible attack that still haunted him. I needed my character to agree to go or else the book would have been rather short, but I had to sit and come up with a legitimate reason. I had to figure out what would motivate him to agree to do something that he normally would not do. And it had to be believable to the reader, which means it had to be believable to my character. Ultimately, I ended up having those who wanted to send my character there playing a tape of radio traffic they had just intercepted indicating some of the members of his team were still alive. Now he had a real, and pressing, reason to go.

Often your protagonist is initially reluctant to get involved, and circumstances force him to do so. Your protagonist also usually begins by reacting, but eventually he must make choices and take action or he will lose reader empathy.

Once you know your characters' motivations, in essence, you lose control of a large portion of the book as the characters begin to act and react according to their personalities. For example, in *Lonesome Dove*, when Blue Duck kidnaps Lori, author Larry McMurtry had little choice on what was going to happen next, given who his characters were. There was no doubt that Gus was going after Lori, that Captain Call was keeping the cattle drive moving north, and that Jake Spoon would go to San Antonio and gamble. Each character acted true to his nature.

CHARACTER TRAITS AND PERSONALITIES

Consider extremes when writing about your characters in order to involve your reader more intensely. You can have a good character and a bad character. But would the reader prefer to see an evil character and a noble character? Think of personalities as a pendulum, and understand that the further you swing that pendulum, the more involved the reader usually will be. Therefore, take any positive trait you can think of and try to find its opposite. Do the reverse. Then use those traits to develop your characters.

You need to study people and also remember that you are not the original mold for mankind. Some people are very different than you and have different value systems. Authors who write good characters understand this very well, much better than the average person.

Everyone has a religion. What that means is that everyone has something he believes in, even if it's not God. To write good characters, you need to know what their values and belief systems are, then keep them acting according to those systems. Even a crazy serial killer character has a belief system, skewed as it may be. In fact, dissecting that belief system is often the way the novel's protagonist catches the killer.

I recommend reading John Douglas's *Mindhunter*. Douglas was one of the founders of the FBI's Investigative Support Unit, which specializes in profiling. A profiler looks at the evidence, then tries to figure out who the person is. An author does the opposite. She invents the person, then comes up with the evidence that is representative of that person. Profiling also shows that people have character traits that dictate their actions.

It may be difficult for you to develop an agenda for a character that is explicitly different from your own. You must keep in mind that the character is not totally aware of his own agenda, thus leaving it up to you to show the reader this agenda.

Be careful when creating a character who is a composite of several people you know. Often, various parts of different personalities don't fit together smoothly in one person. If your parts don't fit together, your character will appear to have multiple personalities. (Maybe that's what you want!) One way to have your character's traits fit together is to use a profiling technique like the one mentioned previously. A character who fits one of the Myers-Briggs personality types I talked about earlier will be a consistent and believable character.

Every character trait is double-edged. Sometimes I read a student's character sketch and ask, "What's wrong with this person? What's bad about him?" Too often the characters are projected as two-dimensional, perfect people. All female characters are beautiful. All male characters are more than six feet tall, know martial arts, are deadly with guns . . . and still loving fathers to their children. Right.

If someone is very loyal, is that a good thing? Can't loyalty carried to an extreme be bad? Isn't that true of every so-called good emotion? Can't love slide into obsession? By working with all sides of an emotion, you add depth and interest to your characters.

Even in an action-oriented book, it is useful for the main character to have an ongoing personal crisis, as a sort of subplot that moves along with the major action crisis. An emotional subplot helps keep the readers as interested in the character as in the plot. However, it's not as easy to do as it sounds. A successful character subplot usually has to do several things:

1. It can't distract the reader and take away from the action of the main plot. Rather, it should supplement it.
2. It should have a conclusion before or at the same time the main plot concludes, unless it is part of a series.
3. It should support the main plot in some manner, beyond the simple fact that the character is involved in the main plot. For example, if your detective is going through a divorce while she is working the big case, is there a way the divorce itself can be connected to the big case beyond the effect it has on the detective? Maybe the prime suspect's lawyer also represents the detective's husband? (I talk more about this in the section on subplots on page 130.)

YOUR CHARACTERS' PSYCHOLOGY

One of the hardest things to do as a writer is to show something about a character rather than tell it. Most people (and characters) are often unaware of the reasons for their own actions. Noted psychologist Abraham Maslow developed a hierarchy of needs that suggests people are motivated by the following unsatisfied needs—see if you can use them to assist you in showing your character's motivation rather than simply telling it:

1. **Physiological:** Basic needs such as air, food, sleep, and water.
2. **Safety:** A need to establish security and stability in chaos.
3. **Social:** A need to belong to groups and escape feelings of loneliness and alienation.
4. **Ego:** A need for self-esteem, attention, and recognition.
5. **Self-actualization:** A need for fulfillment as a person.

To give you an example of how a writer shows something about a character rather than simply telling the reader, let's look at Lisa Alther's book *Kinflicks*. Alther wanted to show how one of the female characters was always greatly influenced by whatever man was in her life. A brilliant writer like me would have said: "And she was greatly influenced by whatever man happened to be living with her that year." Alther shows this by having the woman dress differently each year when she flies home to visit her mother.

Psychology also indicates that people build up their strongest defenses around the weakest parts of their character. This is often called a person's blind spot, and it can cripple a person in pursuit of his goal. Does your character have a blind spot?

Some writing instructors say a main character has to change by the end of the story. How many people do you know who have really changed? The answer gets down to the definition of change and what happens to a character when he undergoes change.

Change occurs when a character has a moment of enlightenment, makes a decision based on that moment, and then has to live with the consequences of that decision, which ultimately does change both the character and the story. The "burning bush" type of change—where everything about the person changes in an instant—is hard to pull off realistically. Most of the time, if you do that type of complete change, it will ring false to the reader, like an author manipulation.

Ninety-nine percent of what people do every day is habit. And habits are extremely difficult to change. A great example of character "change" is in the movie *The Verdict*. Paul Newman plays a drunken, down-and-out lawyer. His only case is a wrongful injury suit. When he's in the hospital taking pictures of a woman in a coma, he suddenly stops and just looks at the woman. There isn't a word of dialogue, but he has a moment of enlightenment. The body in the bed is suddenly not a case but a real person. He decides then that he will try this case and win it.

What's so good, though, is that he's still a bum and a drunk. He still screws things up. He suddenly doesn't become a brilliant, sober lawyer. But with his decision, he does do some things differently, and because he has to live with the results of that decision, he is forced to change. Even better, his decision at first appears to be a very bad one as things immediately begin to go wrong for him.

Consider whether your reader will have empathy for your protagonist. Too often I get character sketches or stories from writers where the main character is someone who the reader won't like. Now, once in a while, a really good writer can pull that off, but it's hard to do. I bring up empathy right after talking about change in a character because sometimes writers want to start with a negative main character and have the character change into a likable one by the end of the book. The difficulty with such a story is getting the reader hooked on a character he might not like. If you try to do this, you should have some sort of redeeming quality scene very early so the reader knows there is a seed of hope.

A good example of this is in Pulitzer prize-winning author Richard Russo's book *Nobody's Fool*. Sully, the protagonist, abandoned his family when his son was very young. At the start, he's a bum without many redeemable features. However, there's a scene early in the book where he is with his landlord and her son. The son wants his mother to kick Sully out of the house because he falls asleep smoking in bed and the son fears the house will burn down. The mother is looking out the window and sees an old, demented woman wandering the street in her bathrobe, walking in the snow. Sully, without putting his shoes on, runs out the door, into the snow, and brings the lady in, treating her nicely. What does this say about his character? What does not stopping to put his shoes on say about him?

In screenwriting, it is generally accepted that within the first ten minutes of the film (i.e., the first ten pages of the screenplay) the nature of the main character has to be shown to the audience in some manner. As a novel writer you should also "set" your main character pretty early in the novel.

Can you look at someone who is different from you, who has different values, and not only understand him, but empathize with him to a certain extent? Many smart people have a hard time understanding characters who do things that are obviously not smart. Yet those same smart people have blind spots in their personalities where they do corresponding not-smart actions. It's difficult as an author to create characters who are oblivious to their faults. You can't spell those faults out to the reader, you have to show them as character traits.

You will always have a protagonist and an antagonist. In *Butch Cassidy and the Sundance Kid*, who is the protagonist?

Butch.

Why? Because he always comes up with the plans.

In *Lonesome Dove*, who is the protagonist? Even though we might love Gus the most, the protagonist is Call, because he keeps the plot moving via the cattle drive. Also, he is the one still standing at the very end, right back where he started.

Remember that your protagonist is only as good as the antagonist is bad. In *Silence of the Lambs*, there would be no Clarice Starling without a Hannibal Lecter.

Try to give your antagonist as strong a motivation as your protagonist so that the conflict between them rings true. Many times I'll get a character sketch from a student, and the antagonist's primary motivation is listed simply as evil. That doesn't work because evil is not a motivator but a result. The antagonist should be developed in such a way that his motivation is understandable to the reader.

Sometimes *less is better*. Occasionally I'll get a manuscript where the main character introduction is followed by his entire life history. How do you feel about meeting someone like that in real life? If you know everything about the person after the first meeting, what's the point in seeing him again?

As the author, you have to know everything about your character, but you don't have to tell the reader everything. A little mystery is intriguing. You know how your character developed a quirky trait, but by not telling the reader up front, you make the reader curious. For example, in the movie *L.A. Confidential*, we meet each of the three main characters in three opening scenes. The characters show us something about who they are by the actions they take, but we don't know *why* they're taking those actions until much further in the movie.

Think about your characters as if they are real people your readers are meeting for the first time on a blind date. Make the meeting memorable.

CHARACTERS AND LITERARY FICTION

I once read a manuscript about a woman, the way her life changed in response to events in it, and her own growing maturity as a person. It made me reevaluate some of the things I've always believed about writing. My focus used to be on action-driven stories because that was what I wrote. That was what I was capable of doing.

Many writers want to write about people, not specifically action. There is nothing wrong with that. However, there are some crucial points to keep in mind in a character-oriented book.

QUALITIES OF GOOD CHARACTERS

1. **Heroic:** They struggle to meet every day challenges or extreme challenges. Either way they show courage and dignity in their battle. They don't have to be nice, but they do have to be good. If you start with a negative character there must be a glimmer of hope in which the reader can discern that she could change for the better.

2. **Believable:** Give them strengths *and* weaknesses. Often it is the latter that readers identify with more. And you must give consistent evidence of these traits, not just show them once.

3. **Sympathetic:** Readers like characters who make things happen, who actively respond to the world around them instead of constantly reacting. Readers don't particularly care for victims. Remember, I said earlier that you get to truly know someone by how he or she reacts in a crisis. In the same manner, characters grab our attention when they face a crisis. Also remember that opposing external traits cause inner conflict.

4. **Memorable:** Think about your favorite book. What do you remember? The characters.

y rounded character has both a need and a flaw connected to every trait.
are examples:

Trait	Need	Flaw
Loyal	To be trusted	Gullible
Adventurous	To experience change	Unreliable
Altruistic	To be loved	Submissive
Tolerant	To have no conflict	No conviction
Decisive	To be in charge	Impetuous
Realistic	To be balanced by events	Can be controlled
Competitive	To achieve goals	Overlooks costs
Idealistic	To find/achieve the best	Naive

When developing your character's traits, fill in the need that drives her and the flaw that brings her to her moment of enlightenment. Usually, the flaw is a blind spot for the character.

You should treat your characters like you would subplots in an action book. For example, don't have a character appear in chapter three if you don't develop and use that character by the end of the novel. Just as all subplots must be tied to the main plot, all your characters must be tied to the main story, which is your main character's development.

Each character must be real and have his own agenda, just like each person in real life has his own agenda, even if it isn't a conscious one. The characters must also be consistent. Connecting all the characters should be an overarching theme.

Also realize that perhaps the greatest flaw most people have is their lack of awareness of *themselves*, never mind others. As I said earlier, true characters are not walking around completely self-actualized. Many times, they are walking around ignorant of their own agenda. Sometimes authors are also ignorant of their own agenda, specifically why they are trying to write a novel.

Character-oriented books often need to be cut down much more than action-oriented books. The narrative may wander a bit because people's lives tend to wander a bit. Now, there are some authors whose style is so good that you like that wandering—say, a Larry McMurtry or Pat Conroy. But for most, less is better.

If you want to write like Lisa Alther, Anne Tyler, Richard Russo, Jane Smiley, Clyde Edgerton, and others, you should read everything you can that they write. You should study the craft of writing, of putting words into sentences, and into paragraphs. You should hone your craft constantly and get feedback from writers who are better than you.

Author Dennis Lehane started as a genre writer and is now rising above the field. His early books are clearly mysteries. However, with *Mystic River*, he took his craft to another level. While a murder mystery is part of the story line, the focus is more on the effect of this murder on the major characters rather than simply resolving the mystery.

The quality of writing in a character-oriented book must be higher because it must evoke strong emotion in the reader, not just intellectual interest. Marketing character-oriented books is also somewhat different, and I touch on that more in chapter nine.

POINT OF VIEW

What is reality? What someone perceives it to be. Keep this in mind in terms of the point of view (POV) you choose to write your novel in, and the points of view of both the reader and your characters.

After many years of writing and teaching novel writing, I firmly believe that perspective or point of view is the number one style problem for most writers. With a bit of awareness of both the problem and possible solutions, it is also one of the easiest problems to correct. For the sake of simplicity, in this section I will stick with the term point of view, although it is interchangeable with perspective.

When considering how to tell your story, the first thing you have to do is select a point of view. This is a key step in transitioning from idea to story. Often the type of story you are writing will dictate the point of view, but a good understanding of the various modes of presentation is essential—this is one area where beginning novelists often have problems. While they may select the right point of view, it is often used poorly because of a lack of understanding of the tool itself.

Regardless of which point of view (or points of view) you choose to use, you, as the author, must feel good about the point of view with which you are telling the story. If you don't have a warm and fuzzy feeling about that, this confusion will most definitely be translated to the reader. Remember, ultimately, point of view is your voice as a writer.

Some people write like an MTV music video: point of view flying all over the place, giving glimpses into each character but never really keeping the reader oriented. I say this because the best analogy I can give for point of view is to look at it as your camera. You are the director: You see and know everything in your story. But the reader only sees and knows what the camera records from its unique perspective: the point of view you choose. While you see the entire scene, your lens only records the words you put on the page, and you have to keep your lens tightly focused and firmly in hand.

Like a director, you must know when to "cut." A cut in film terminology is when the camera is either: (1) stopped, then restarted later, either in the same place or in a new place; or (2) stopped and another camera, with a different perspective is then used. To a writer, a cut is a change in point of view. With point of view, you have to keep the reader oriented about what camera he is seeing the scene through. The reader has to know from what point of view he is viewing the scene. Lose that and you lose the reader. There is no wrong point of view, or even mixture of point of views, to write in, but be careful not to confuse the reader as to the point of view through which he is "seeing" the story.

Let's take the camera analogy a bit further. When directors do a scene, they immediately look into a viewfinder and watch the recording of the take. They do this because, although they saw what happened, they have to know what the camera recorded. As an author, you have to get out of your own point of view and be able to see what you write as the reader sees it. All that counts for the reader is what you have written down, not what you think you have written down.

While there are a number of modes of point of view, the three most common in novels are first person, third person, and omniscient.

FIRST-PERSON POINT OF VIEW

First person means you use the word "I" quite a bit. With first-person point of view, you're giving the camera to one character and letting her film a documentary while doing a voiceover.

First person has its advantage in that the narrator is telling her own story. The major disadvantage is that the reader can only see and know what the narrator knows. The narrator can be a witness or a participant in the story. You, as the author, are absent in this mode, thus you surrender part of your control in writing. Remember, the first-person narrator is not you the author but rather the character in the story.

Note that there are certain genres that fit first person very well, most particularly mysteries. By using first person, the mystery writer can bring the reader along for the ride, disclosing clues as the narrator discovers them.

The major disadvantage of first person is that your narrator has to be present in every scene. Because of this, many writers make their narrator the protagonist. Another problem can be the logistics of getting your narrator to all the key events in order to narrate them. Inexperienced writers can end up with very convoluted and unrealistic plots. If the narrator isn't present at these important scenes, then she has to find out about them by other means, which can lessen suspense and definitely lessen the immediacy of the action in the story since you have major action occurring offstage.

Some authors use a narrator who isn't one of the main characters, someone who is more of an observer. This type of narrator is known as a detached narrator. Using a detached narrator has some advantages. Think of the Sherlock Holmes stories. Who is narrating? Watson. Why? Because this allows Sir Arthur Conan Doyle to withhold what Holmes is thinking from the audience.

Another question to think about when using a first-person point of view: Should the reader believe your narrator? If everything your narrator says is fact, then there might not be much suspense. But think about the movie *The Usual Suspects*. The story is narrated by a character who turns out to be the man everyone is searching for, thus he has been lying from the very beginning of his narration. In a book, you can raise suspense if your first person narrator is caught in a small lie early on in the story—the reader will then have to be more judgmental about everything else the narrator says.

When using first-person narration, you also need to consider tense and time. There are two ways to view time in a first-person story:

1. *I remember when.* The narrator is telling the story in past tense, looking backward. This way immediately reduces the suspense of whether the narrator survives the story. The narrator is also withholding information from the reader—she obviously

knows the ending, yet chooses not to reveal it.

2. *In real time.* The narrator is telling the story as it unfolds around him. What happens when the narrator is involved in an emotionally overwhelming event? Will he still be able to narrate the story?

Keeping the type of time frame consistent within a story can be a challenge. Even the best of writers tend to slip from real time to past time.

When using first person, be careful not to slide into second-person point of view. Any time you put *you* in your narrative while addressing the reader, you have moved from first to second person. You should avoid doing that because it breaks the consistency of the narrative.

There are ways to get around the disadvantages of first person.

A WORD ABOUT SECOND-PERSON POINT OF VIEW

Second person has been used in novels, but it is difficult to work with. Second person uses "you" or "we" in telling the story. It can bring the reader into the story more intimately, in fact, making the reader part of the story in the role of participant or close observer.

TEST: What point of view is this book in?

ANSWER: Second person. Why did I choose that point of view? That's easy—because I wanted you to be involved when you read it. I wanted you, the reader, to feel that I was talking directly to you.

Overall, though, second person rarely is used in a novel because it implies that the reader is part of the story.

Examine some first-person novels, and you will discover them. *Interview With the Vampire* by Anne Rice is an interesting and brilliant use of first person. The title tells you why. The story starts with a first-person narrative by a reporter who is preparing to interview a vampire. The bulk of the book consists of the interview—the vampire Louis's first-person narrative of his life. Rice can go back in time with Louis and then return to the present with the reporter, both in first person. She has two levels of interest and suspense: the present fate of the narrator and the fate of the vampire in his own tale.

I watch videos and read books in a different mode as a "writer." I study them for structure, to see what the author, screenwriter, or director does with the subject matter, how it is presented. When you pick up a novel, the first thing you should note is what point of view is being used. Then ask yourself why the author chose that point of view. What did the novel gain from that point of view?

One last note about first person: It is the voice most novice writers naturally gravitate to, but it is one of the most difficult voices to do well. Because of that, there is an initial negative impression among agents and editors when confronted with a first-person story.

In the examples starting on page 117, you will see more clearly the advantages and disadvantages of first person.

THIRD-PERSON POINT OF VIEW

Third-person point of view allows the author to be like a movie camera moving to any set and recording any event, as long as one of the characters is lugging the camera. It also allows the camera to slide behind the eyes of any character, but beware—do it too often or awkwardly, and you will lose your reader very quickly. When using third person, don't get in your characters' heads to show the reader their thoughts, but rather let their actions and words lead the reader to figure those thoughts out.

Third Person Locked. If you stay with just one character in a novel, and everything is seen from that one point of view, it may seem like you should be writing a first-person novel. However, many writers employ a locked third-person point of view (not switching to any other character) in order to create distance from the main character. The author might not want a first-person voiceover. Michael Connelly's Harry Bosch books, such as *Angel's Flight* or *Trunk Music,* employ this point of view. While time is an issue in first person, distance is an issue in third person. How close does the author get to each character? How much of her inner thoughts are revealed? This distance is the difference between being in third-person point of view and omniscient. An omniscient narrator can get into any character's head but from outside in, not inside out. Thus, the point of view of the novel can "see beyond" a character's own flaws and deluded perceptions. Omniscient is a good choice if you're looking for such flexibility, but an unreliable third-person point of view is what some books are entirely built on. It is all a question of what you are trying to achieve.

Third Person Shifting. When you are in third person, everything that happens is filtered through the five senses of the character whose point of view you are in at the moment. The character, in effect, *is* the camera. In contrast to third person locked, which allows one person to be the camera, third person shifting allows more than one character to be the camera, as the narrative shifts between different characters.

There is a strong tendency, especially when first starting out, to employ third person shifting. While this is the most common and accepted mode of third-person point of view in novels, it also presents several problems if handled poorly.

Third person shifting can cause readers to wonder whose head they are in during a scene, unless you make the cuts clear. Some writers avoid this confusion by changing the character POV with each chapter. The reader then grows to expect a different character POV each time they start a new chapter.

Larry McMurtry is a master of point of view. In some places in *Comanche Moon,* the last book in the Lonesome Dove series, he changes third person POV almost every paragraph. However, Larry McMurtry also won the Pulitzer prize. Most of us aren't that good. He succeeds because he is able to completely change his writing style for each character so that you immediately know and feel that you are seeing the scene from that specific character's unique point of view. For example, in one scene the Texas Ranger, Gus, and the Native American, Famous Feet, are walking in the desert. They spot a mound of buffalo skulls. In one paragraph, through Gus's point of view, we get his reaction to the mound. In the next paragraph, we get Famous Feet's completely different reaction to seeing the same exact thing. Each man sees the skulls differently because of his background. Gus sees the skulls from the white man's perspective of hunting. For Famous Feet, however, the skulls represent the end of his people's way of life. For an additional example of third person shifting, see page 120.

You cheat the reader if you are constantly in your characters' heads, yet you hold back something the characters know (which is sometimes necessary for your suspense). Try to keep a consistent depth of insight into each character's thoughts.

When using third person shifting, you will, by the nature of the POV, most likely give each character's viewpoint on various topics, most especially other characters. However, use them carefully. Multiple viewpoints can be confusing to the reader who has his own viewpoint of the story you have presented so far. You also might confuse the reader if the characters have disagreeing points of view. Such disagreement is normal if the characters are realistic, and it can be an advantage *if handled well*—differing points of view on the same scene can make for intriguing reading.

All the above is not to say don't get inside your characters' heads—indeed, as I mentioned it is the most common form in published books—but when you do it, do it carefully. Keep the number of characters whose viewpoint you present to a minimum. When you go into a character's mind, the reader assumes that the character is as essential to the plot as every other character whose point of view you have taken. You should spend an equal amount of time on every character whose point of view you use.

Make sure cuts between characters' points of view are clear. As I mentioned earlier, one way to do that is to stick with one character for each section or chapter of the novel so that when the reader flips the page to a new chapter she begins to expect being in another character's head. Remember that if you stay with your characters' points of view, you are controlling the lenses through which readers see the story unfold. You must be very careful with that control because you are controlling the reality the reader sees.

If you choose to employ third person shifting, consider what you are going to do when two or three characters whose points of view you use are going to be in the same scene. Are you going to shift from one to the other? Or stay with one? If you stick with one, the reader may wonder what the other characters think and feel. Try to limit the number of points of view you take in order to strengthen select characters in your story.

OMNISCIENT POINT OF VIEW

Also known as authorial narrative, I liken omniscient point of view to the camera getting pulled back in order to show the viewer more. As I mentioned earlier, there are times you might want to pull back so you can tell the reader more information or show the reader more than the characters who are in the scene might be able to see or know.

For example, if you want a reader to simply understand a battle scene, omniscient point of view is a good choice. The camera is pulled back and able to show just the action without slowing down to process it through a character's five senses, thoughts, and emotions. But if you want the reader to see how one specific character is responding to the danger of combat, you might stick with third person from that character's point of view. For a successful example of omniscient point of view, read Richard Russo, the winner of the 2002 Pulitzer prize for *Empire Falls*.

Third Person Vs. Omniscient. It's easy to confuse third person with omniscient. I use omniscient for expository information that would be awkward to continually push through a third person POV, but I move to third person to give more depth to my characters and give their reactions and thoughts to situations.

Here is the difference between an expository scene in third person limited and omniscient:

» **Third person**

Joe walked up the dirt road leading to the Giza Plateau. As he cleared the rise he saw the Sphinx off to his right and the three massive pyramids ahead. He knew that historians believed the largest of the three had been built by the Pharaoh Khufu, more popularly known as Cheops. He'd read that it was 138 meters high. He was impressed with the magnitude of the construction, noting the massive blocks of aged stone and wondering how they had been moved so long ago.

» **Omniscient**

Joe walked up the dirt road leading to the Giza Plateau. The Sphinx was to his right and the three massive pyramids in front. Historians believe the largest pyramid was built by the Pharaoh Khufu, more popularly known as Cheops. The largest pyramid is 138 meters high, built of massive blocks of aged stone that must have taken a marvel of engineering to move.

The second presents the information directly, without processing it through Joe's head. If you want to break yourself of always using a character's point of view, try using the word *the* to start sentences. This will help you in writing narrative. Remember that you are the author. You can actually write down what you want to say without having it come from the point of view of one of your characters.

POINT OF VIEW EXAMPLES

You have to consider point of view before you begin your book and before you write every scene, much as a movie director does. You must determine the best point of view to convey to the reader the story you are trying to tell.

Say you are going to write a thriller about a female FBI agent tracking down a vicious serial killer. You want to open your book with a scene that will grab the reader and set the stage for the suspense of the novel, so you decide to open with a killing. What point of view will you use? Now, remember, no point of view is *wrong*—you just have to understand the advantages and disadvantages of your choices and make a knowledgeable decision.

First person might be a bit difficult. After all, this would most likely mean your narrator actually witnesses the opening scene. This isn't impossible, but it could be awkward. Perhaps you use first person from the protagonist's point of view, and she witnesses the murder but is not in a position to take any action. If you use first person from the killer's point of view, then your book will be from that point of view. If you use first person from the victim's point of view, then you have a very short book, unless the victim survives.

You can decide to use third person from the point of view of the victim. This can build tension, but it also means the chapter will end abruptly. You can use third person from the point of view of the killer, but remember that the killer knows who he is and therefore you have to be careful how much insight into the killer's head you allow. A technique some writers use to overcome that limitation is to have the killer think of himself in different terms other than his reality. The killer is Joe Schmo, but when he's in killer mode he thinks of himself as Doctor Death, thus hiding his identity from the reader.

Or, you could use omniscient, placing your "camera" above the scene. Here, though, you have to be careful not to show too much and give away the killer's identity. Much like a director might choose a dark basement where the viewer can't see the killer's face, you will do the same. Doing it in the middle of a Kansas wheat field at high noon might give away too much.

Or, perhaps you have two characters meeting in a pub for an important exchange of dialogue. They sit across from each other. How are you going to "shoot" this scene? From third person via one of the characters? That means you get that character's thoughts, and you describe the other character's reactions through the first character's senses—i.e., the camera is on your POV character's shoulder. Is it important that the reader know one character's thoughts more than the other character's? Or is it more important to show one character's reactions more than the other's?

Or, do you keep switching the camera back and forth across the booth, going from one to the other? Be careful though, as such switching is very disconcerting to the reader. Or do you shoot it omniscient with the camera off to the side showing actions and recording dialogue, with the option of adding authorial narrative?

Consider this scene like a date. If you were out with someone and you knew exactly what he or she was thinking, and you knew what you were thinking, would there be any suspense to the date? Taking too many points of view can greatly reduce your suspense.

For examples of the various points of view try to visualize the following: Your point of view character, Joe, is sitting in a room looking out a window into a courtyard. Two men walk into the courtyard, speaking to each other. They proceed to get into a fight. Notice the various ways I can write this scene:

1. First person.

I saw the two people walk into the courtyard. They began to argue with each other, and then suddenly, they began to fight.

Note: Because I wasn't out there, I couldn't hear what they said, which is a limitation of first person. However, I could find out what was said later on by talking to one of the two people. (There are always ways to get around disadvantages.) Or, I could change the story and have my first person character in the courtyard in order to be able to relate what happens—but the presence of that character in the courtyard could also change what occurs. My narrator would also be unable to identify the two men unless he knew them.

If I changed the story and made my narrator one of the fighting men, then I'd need to decide whether I am telling this as it occurs or looking back. If I am telling as it occurs, then can my narrator still narrate what is happening coherently while in the middle of participating in a fight?

2. **Third person, locked point of view.** You are telling the reader what is happening from Joe's point of view, and he knows something about what is happening:

Joe saw Chris walk into the courtyard with Ted. Joe could see that they were arguing, and he knew they were still probably upset about their earlier confrontation over Madeline's boyfriend.

He saw Chris hold up his hands in a placating manner and say something. Then he noticed that Ted was yelling something back, and Chris dropped his hands.

Joe jumped to his feet as he saw Chris grab the collar of Ted's windbreaker.

Everything that happens is being filtered through Joe's senses. And we have to trust Joe's assumptions about the scene; for example, that the two are upset over the earlier confrontation. For all Joe knows, it might be something very different.

Many writers overcome trusting only one character by switching POVs from one character to another who has a better camera angle.

3. **Third person, shifting point of view.** In the same scene as above, we start in Joe's point of view, and then shift when it is necessary.

Joe looked up from his cup of coffee and saw Chris and Ted walk into the courtyard. Joe could see that they were arguing, and he knew they were still probably upset about their earlier confrontation over Madeline's boyfriend.

In the courtyard, Chris could see Joe watching them, but he could care less. Chris was still uneasy about the fight over Madeline's boyfriend.

"I still don't accept it," Ted muttered. "It's wrong."

Chris held up his hands. "I don't want to talk about it any more. We've discussed Philip enough. It's up to Madeline."

"No, it's not up to Madeline. We have a responsibility. He's not good for her, and I don't approve of them going out together."

Chris dropped his hands and glared at Ted; he could never just let anything go. "I said, I don't want to talk about it again. Period."

Ted looked at him. "We have to. I think . . . "

Chris felt something snap inside of him, and he grabbed the collar of Ted's windbreaker. "Goddamn it. I told you I didn't want to talk about it again."

Here I describe what is happening in the courtyard by getting into one of the two men's heads. Note that I make sure the reader knows I've shifted character POV by reversing the camera angle. I let the reader know a background by having one of the characters thinking about it. We can hear what is said, and we know what the argument is about. The camera is on Chris's shoulder with a feed into his brain. We know who the characters are because Chris, the POV character, knows. We also know that what Joe suspected was true, by having Chris confirm what they were fighting about.

How do you let a reader know the POV has shifted in third person? The subject of the sentence identifies the POV.

4. **Omniscient (author as narrator).** Here the author simply records observations, showing, not telling:

Chris and Ted walked into the courtyard. Ted's face was tight, his forehead wrinkled in thought, his eyes smoldering. "I still don't accept it. It's wrong."

Chris held up his hands. "I don't want to talk about it any more. We've discussed Philip enough. It's up to Madeline."

"No, it's not up to Madeline. We have a responsibility. He's not good for her, and I don't approve of them going out together."

Chris dropped his hands and glared at Ted. "I said, I don't want to talk about it again. Period."

Ted wasn't to be dissuaded. "We have to. I think—"

Chris's hands shot up, and his fingers wrapped around the collar of Ted's windbreaker. "Goddamn it. I told you I didn't want to talk about it again."

I manage to impart all the information needed and describe the scene. In this mode, you can make authorial comments such as Ted not being dissuaded because, as the author, you know what everyone is thinking.

You could also write this scene with an omniscient point of view and give *both* characters' thoughts and inner reactions.

Note that in first person, because I had the glass window between the characters, and me/Joe, I couldn't hear what Ted and Chris said. If I put myself in the courtyard with them, my presence might affect the action. In third person I am free to lock onto either one of the characters. In omniscient I am floating overhead, and not affecting the scene at all.

Every time you use a point of view, make sure you look at the advantages and disadvantages. Recognize what information you are imparting and ultimately try to see things from the reader's point of view. In the final analysis, you must make sure the information you want your reader to have is smoothly imparted.

Please don't think from all that I have written above that it is wrong to get in your characters' heads. If you go into the bookstore today and pull the top ten fiction novels off the shelf, I think more than half would probably have varying degrees of insight into the characters' thoughts and feelings. The key is to do it right. As long as you use the tool properly, you will be all right.

Remember: consistency and smoothness. Make sure the reader knows where the "camera" is.

MIXING POINT OF VIEW IN THE SAME NOVEL

Remember my premise: There is no wrong way. Yes, mixing point of view in the same novel can be done. A certain fellow named William Faulkner did an okay job of it in a novel called *The Sound and the Fury*. The first three sections of that book were first person (indeed, three very different first persons). The last third person. You can do anything that works. It certainly worked for Faulkner, but remember, smoothness.

When you watch a TV show or a film, start paying very close attention how the director filmed the scene. Think about something as simple as two people sitting in a booth at a restaurant. Does the director film it from the side, showing both people? Or does the camera shift back and forth from one side of the table to the other? And if it shifts, when do the shifts take place? Does the director want to show the person speaking, or the person listening and reacting to the other's words?

Do you see how many different ways a scene can be filmed?

DIALOGUE

Psychologists say that a very large percentage of communication is nonverbal, yet on the printed page all you have are your words. They aren't accompanied by the tone of your voice, your facial expressions, or hand gestures—nothing that in normal face-to-face communication can drastically affect the message being communicated. Because all you have are the words, you must choose them very carefully. A conversation in a novel is *not* exactly as it would be in real life. You must be careful not to bore the reader; your written dialogue will usually be more concise than a spoken conversation.

PURPOSES OF DIALOGUE

You use dialogue for many reasons beyond the simple fact that your plot calls for conversation at certain points. Dialogue is a good way to overcome limitations of some of the other tools you are using. For example, if you are writing a first-person detective story, dialogue is useful in giving your main character (and in turn the reader) important information. It can impart backstory information and exposition.

Dialogue can reveal a great amount of information about your characters. It is their chance to express themselves directly to the reader. Dialogue can reveal motivations, which is critical to character. Remember, though, just like in real life you have to consider whether what a person says is the truth. Is your character telling the truth?

Make sure the voice of each character is consistent. If you want to check this, review what you've written, and highlight everything each character says, using different colors for the different characters. Then trace each character's dialogue by itself, making sure it is the same voice. Also, make sure that your characters don't sound the same.

Dialogue also advances the plot. It can sharpen conflict between characters. It can be used to control the pace of the story. Sometimes if you are going full speed ahead with action, dialogue is a good way to slow things down and give the reader a breather. But more often it creates suspense and intensifies the conflict in the story.

Movies always tend to search for that greater line. Who can forget Clint Eastwood's "Go ahead, make my day"? While your dialogue should keep the readers' attention, be wary of stilted dialogue.

Dialogue must fit the characters, but try to avoid excessive slang as it usually interrupts the smoothness even though it is natural for that character and locale. Think about it: Readers are going along, your smooth prose has them absorbed in the story, and all of sudden the writing changes to slang. It can be disconcerting. Again there are places where it works, but understand what the disadvantage is and weigh it before using.

Don't overuse dialogue. Even in a screenplay, half the page should be action. If your book starts to exceed fifty percent dialogue you might have too much, although, as usual there are exceptions to this.

DIALOGUE TAGS

Any words you use to indicate who is speaking is a dialogue tag. Many new writers may feel they have to use terms such as "he exclaimed," "she gasped," and "he shrieked," to make up for a lack of tone or gestures. It can be, and often is, overdone. Use strong dialogue tags when absolutely necessary, but don't overuse them or they will take away from the other words. The placement of the dialogue tag is also important. It should be either at the front, middle, or end of the *first* sentence of dialogue. Don't have an entire paragraph of dialogue and then at the end of the fifth sentence put a comma and quotation marks and "Joe said." If you do that, the reader spends five sentences wondering exactly who is speaking.

If you have more than one male in a scene you shouldn't use "he," even if in the context of the writing it's pretty evident who is speaking. Same with more than one female. It might not be evident to readers who's speaking. Also, don't forget about bystanders in a scene, and don't let readers forget about them. I've read scenes with three people in them, where one says nothing and sort of fades into nothingness, and then startlingly reappears at the end with a snippet of dialogue.

Dialogue is usually much shorter in a novel than it would be in

OTHER DIALOGUE POINTS

1. I said previously that you can use dialogue to give expository information but if you do it too obviously, then guess what—the reader will notice and be distracted. For example, Jim turns to his wife, Marge, and says: "Gee, Marge, your Uncle Bill, the famous artist, is coming from his home in France, to visit us next week." Now, you did give the reader important information about Bill here: he's an artist, Marge's uncle, and lives in France. But, wouldn't Marge know her own uncle is an artist and lives in France? Do it another way.

2. Although dialogue in a novel is usually much more concise and to the point than dialogue in real life, be sure it doesn't appear stilted or formal. Your characters can use contractions.

3. Use caution when using quotation marks to delineate a character's thoughts. You risk confusing the reader, who naturally assumes quotation marks mean dialogue. Also, if you are writing in third person, how do you draw the line between those thoughts that go inside the quotation marks and everything else in narrative, which to a certain extent is also from a character's point of view? And finally, such a technique is telling not showing. Instead, try putting a character's thoughts in italics, or perhaps she could say them aloud.

4. While you should be wary of dialogue tags, there are times when you have to get across more emotion or attitude than the words themselves can convey. Make up for the lack with action and setting rather than dialogue tags. Also, there are times in extended conversations where readers can get so caught up in the dialogue they lose track of the environment around the characters. You should occasionally throw in a bit of action in the midst of your dialogue. For example, when you are talking to

someone on the phone, do you sit totally still? Or do you move about? When you talk to your boss, does he sit like a statue on the other side of his desk and respond to your questions like Data on *Star Trek: The Next Generation*? Keep the reader oriented to where the characters are and what the characters are doing. You can give more emphasis to your dialogue by having the characters make movements or gestures, but don't overdo it.

5. You can use dialogue to give expository information that is necessary for the story, but beware of slowing your action down too much. Consider using your author's voice to give narrative information instead of contriving scenes where your characters have to sit around and discuss something in order to give that information to the reader. (I should know this as I just got an editorial letter back on one of my books with just this point.)

6. If you have only two characters in a scene, the reader knows when they hit an end quotation mark that they are going to the other character; however, you should only do about three or four exchanges like that before reorienting the reader as to who is speaking. We've all read scenes where we had to go back up and count the end quote marks to figure out who is talking. Don't make the reader work that hard.

7. Keep the story flowing. Don't stop the story to let your characters have a discussion and then jump-start it at the end of the discussion.

real life. In real-life conversation, people expend numerous words to make a point. In print, these extra words would quickly cause the reader to lose interest. A book such as Nicholson Baker's *Vox*, however, which revolves around phone conversations, naturally will include a higher degree of dialogue than other books might.

SETTING

Setting establishes mood. Go to the bookstore, open up a bunch of books, and read the first line. You will find the majority of opening sentences have something to do with setting and evoking an emotion in the reader. For many novels, setting is one of the two major aspects that make one particular book distinctive from another, the other being character. Setting can help you answer the critical question that usually comes after your original idea: What makes your book different from all the other similar ones?

Setting can be a character in your story. In Jon Krakauer's *Into Thin Air*, Mount Everest and the weather function as antagonists. Some writers have totally wrapped their story around their setting, and it's what makes their book unique. Caleb Carr's stories are mysteries set in New York City in the late nineteenth century, and it is the setting that sets them apart from other mysteries.

Next time you're watching your favorite sitcom or TV drama, pay attention when the scene shifts. In *NYPD Blue*, every time the scene shifts back to the station house, don't they show the outside of the building for a second or so before moving inside? Ever wonder why the director does that? He does it to orient you as the viewer. As a writer, you also have to keep your reader oriented.

Setting consists of the where and the when of your story. And there is so much more to the where than most people see at first glance. Think about the different places you've lived (if you've lived in different places). More than the location was different. Weren't the people somewhat different? The weather? The socioeconomic structure? The seasons? The physical terrain? The architecture? Don't get caught up in simply describing what a place looks like. It takes much more than that to make it come alive.

I have found this to be particularly true in writing science fiction.

Maybe it's simply because I've become more aware of the entirety of the setting when I can't take anything for granted. When my main character steps through a portal and gets sucked into the fourth dimension, I suddenly become much more aware that I have to describe *everything* down to the very texture of the air they breathe.

However (you knew there was a however coming, didn't you?), like everything else in writing, you just can't slam the brakes on your plot and wax eloquently about the fierce north wind roaring through your chapter. It has to come when the reader needs to know about it.

How much is too much detail? If you can take it out and the reader won't miss it.

One other technique I do highly recommend is called "set," short

SYMBOLISM

Remember those literature classes where the teacher went on about Faulkner's use of the color yellow in *Soldiers' Pay*? Did she call it symbolism?

In the opening of Richard Russo's superb book *Nobody's Fool,* several pages are spent on the old trees overlooking the main street in the town the story is set in. The trees were once the pride of the main street, but now they are old and diseased, and the people who live there fear them, worried that an unexpected branch will collapse on their homes. The trees symbolize a large theme in the novel, as they represent the way the entire town has decayed.

Sometimes action can be bluntly symbolic of a character's feelings. Sully hates his departed father. Every time he drives by the cemetery where his father is buried, Sully gives the grave the finger.

Symbolism is one way writers *show* things to the reader, rather than tell them.

for "set the scene." When you start a new chapter or change perspective, you have to quickly (usually in the first two paragraphs) orient the reader by answering:

» Where is the locale?
» When in the timeline does this scene occur, particularly in relation to the previous scene?
» What is the point of view, and if it is a character's, which character?
» Who is here?

Answering those questions "sets" the scene.

SUBPLOTS

Subplots are everything in your story other than your main story line. To make a strong story, all the subplots should connect back to the main story line. Remember the story graph in chapter five. Note that all the subplots (the thinner lines) eventually move back into the main story line and stay there. (Don't let them wander off again and not come back).

Don't have loose ends. If you put something in your story, make sure it serves a purpose and that you resolve it by the end of the book. Don't put things in your novel just because they are neat or you like writing about them. And use everything you do put in as much as possible. The best stories are very tightly woven with almost every single occurrence, fact, and character serving multiple purposes in keeping the story going.

Don't write something only to make a point or just move the story along. Sometimes you get to a place where you need to present a scene or action to keep the story going; spend some time and make the scene or action have more than one connection to the original idea. Have it serve multiple purposes.

Chekov once said: "Don't have a gun in Act One unless you fire it by Act Three." This is true of writing. Don't throw superfluous things into your story. The reader doesn't know the significance of whatever you write so he assumes that *everything* is significant. You disappoint your reader if you have a scene that appears to be important, but you never refer back to it, and wrote it only to keep your action moving.

When reading manuscripts for critique, I have often been misled because I misjudged the importance of something in early chapters that is never mentioned again. In one case a writer had a large explosion occurring that destroyed quite a bit of property and killed many people. I assumed that this explosion was tied into the main plot; in fact, I figured that the "bad guys" had caused the explosion. For the next fifty pages, I kept anticipating a reference back to that explosion. Yet the explosion was never mentioned again nor really explained. The author had simply used it to set up the circumstances causing the hero to have to use a different escape route. To keep suspense and different levels of intrigue, you should present an event or object, and allow the reader to make the "casual" inference. Yet you know there is a more complex level with a different purpose that eventually will be unveiled and cause the reader to look back and say, "Oh, yeah." Take, for instance, Pat Conroy's *The Lords of Discipline.* In one scene, the main character is in his roommate's father's study talking to the father when he sees the man's journals on the bookcase. A minor observation there, as the conversation is the focus of that scene. Later, however, the journals turn out to be extremely significant when the main character breaks in the office to read them and discovers the truth that brings about the conclusion to the book.

In my book *Cut-Out,* the primary purpose of chapter two is to introduce my main character, Riley. Since he is not yet involved in the crisis (introduced in chapter one), I have to introduce him outside of the main story line. I do this by having him in as exciting a situation as possible (to keep the reader hooked). In that chapter I also start the following supplementary loops:

» I introduce another character who will have a role to play later.
» I introduce a tactical situation and have Riley react to it. In and of itself, this situation only appears to introduce Riley. Yet, some of the factors in this situation will come into play later in the novel when Riley faces other situations and reacts in a similar manner.
» I introduce Riley's relationship with the main female character by having him get a letter from her. We learn about both of the characters and their relationship when he reads the letter.

What could have been a pretty straightforward chapter, simply introducing my main character, now serves multiple purposes, some of which will only become visible to the reader as he gets further into the story.

Every character, incident, location—everything—you put into your novel has to be examined very carefully. What additional use can you make of it? The more uses you can make of each subplot, the tighter the story. The tighter the story, the better the manuscript.

BALANCING PLOTS AND SUBPLOTS

Be careful of having a subplot that is bigger than your original idea or main plot. I once looked at a manuscript where one of the subplots involved the assassination of the President of the United States. While this subplot certainly moved the main plot along, it also kept me wondering how it was going to be resolved to the point of distracting me from the author's main story line.

Remember the narrative structure and my beating home the concept of being able to state your story idea in one sentence? There is only *one* main story with its main crisis, climax, and resolution. Everything else must support that story. Sometimes beginning writers get carried away and overwhelm themselves with subplots to the point where the main idea gets lost. In most cases the writer gets lost writing it, and the reader will certainly be lost reading it.

When in doubt use the KISS technique: Keep It Simple, Stupid.

For a good example of an extremely tightly written book, try reading *A Thousand Acres*, by Jane Smiley, which won the National Book Award. Or try *The General's Daughter*, by Nelson DeMille.

A method I use to keep a handle on my subplots is in Appendix F. List major characters across the top, and go down the page in chronological order, playing out each one's actions. Then draw arrows, lining up the order between these subplots in the manner in which they occur. By the time you reach the resolution, you should find that all your characters have reached the same place (or have died along the way).

This sort of visual outline allows you to keep your subplots from unraveling from the main plot. It also allows you to properly sequence your story, having events happen in the correct order.

I mentioned earlier in this book the power of the subconscious, but let me give you an example of where it can play a role. You will find in your manuscript that you plant seed. You put things into the story that might not necessarily seem important at the time—minor things, like the journals in the Pat Conroy scene I described earlier. Later on, when you get to a part of the book where you're stuck, go back, look for these seeds, and grow them into solutions. When you encounter a problem, many times the answer is in the earlier pages of the book as seeds.

There are three possible scenarios for how Pat Conroy planned for that scene while writing *The Lords of Discipline*. Examine these three because you will see it gives you *three* ways to use subplots and to rewrite:

1. Conroy knew from the very beginning that those journals would be the key that unlocks the answers to the mystery his main character was trying to uncover. In that case, Conroy wrote the journals in when he got to the scene in the study, and when his main character needed to find a key, Conroy already knew what he was going to use.

2. Conroy wrote the journals into the study as part of giving the reader the setting and telling the reader something about the character of the roommate's father. (What do you think of a man who would keep such journals?) When the main character got to the point in the book where he needed a key to unlock the mystery, Conroy found himself working with the same information his main character had. Conroy, as the author, went back through the book, searching, as the main character would, for a key. When he reread what he had written—voilà—he realized, as his main character did, that the journals were the key. Conroy then had his main character break in and read the journals. In this scenario, Conroy's subconscious gave him the answer before he knew what the question was.

3. There were no journals in the study the first time Conroy wrote this scene. He got to the point where his main character needed a key. Conroy thought about it and realized—voilà—he would put the key in the study in the form of the journals. So he went back and wrote them in, thus planting the seed for the flower he would need later on. This is part of the ongoing rewriting process that every author must do as a book progresses.

I don't know which of these actually occurred. The point is that every writer uses *all three* techniques when writing.

→TOOL: 7

YOUR FINESSE

THE WRITING CYCLE

Before we focus on editing, let's review the continuous four-stage cycle that is novel writing.

Stage 1: The idea. You need to know where you are starting each time you sit down to write. Where is the story at that point, and where is it going in the immediate future? Try to do this a chapter or two ahead at a time, always remembering your one sentence original idea.

Stage 2: Research. Upon researching an idea you'll find that there are many other aspects to the subject that you were not aware of. In many cases research drives the creative train. There is a very thin line between being realistic and telling a story. Real life can be pretty amazing and sometimes you only have to bend reality a little for the sake of your story. Bend it too far though, and no one will be interested in sticking with you. Also, you must make sure you have internal validity to your story. For example, if you are writing science fiction and have faster than light space travel, you must have certain rules as to how that travel works, and you must stay within the boundaries of the rules you set up. Remember the plot diagram in chapter five? Research is key to building that background box. I research even while I am writing because it gives me more opportunities to develop the plot. Part of research is doing a book dissection.

Stage 3: Writing. Sit down and write. Start with your outline. Then get into the book itself. Just get it down on paper. The first draft almost always looks awful. But at least it's written. Give yourself a pat on the back for completing a first draft. Worry about the awful later.

Stage 4: Editing. Now, it's time to deal with the awful. Go back and look at what you wrote. Clean it up. Throw it out if it doesn't fit. (But don't literally throw it out. Don't ever discard something you wrote. You never know when you might need it, whether it's after the first draft of the manuscript is completed, or if it's in another story. Label it and save it.) Begin your writing day by rereading what you wrote the previous day, cleaning it up as you go. This technique helps you edit the work and gets you in the proper groove to continue.

Now I am going to be very honest with you. Unlike most writers (or at least unlike what most writers say), I have no real set routine. Sometimes I wake up and jump right into writing. Sometimes I spend days editing. Sometimes I spend days doing nothing but spinning wheels in my head, trying to figure out what I'm doing with the story. (But there are less and less of those days lately because—you got it— I have good outlines.)

There is no typical workday for me other than the fact that I do work at something. I have used all the routines and suggestions in this book at one time or another. But I don't believe in a golden rule of writing routines. If one day you want to write standing on your head on the New York City subway, then go for it (just be careful—it's a jungle out there). Sometimes I sit down and outline chapters just like I suggested in the outlining section. Sometimes I just begin writing it. Do whatever works. But work.

EDITING

Editing is a right-brain, left-brain issue. As physiological psychologists will tell you, the right brain is considered more creative (generally), while the left brain is more logical. Most people consider editing to be a left-brain process, but we do our brains a great disservice if we don't trust our right brains. Many struggling writers use their left brain to dominate their right and devastate their writing.

STORY EDITING

Ask the following questions when editing:

- » Is there continuity?
- » Does the story flow logically?
- » Do these words have a purpose?
- » Do they relate to my story?
- » Should I tell this now, or should some of it wait?
- » Is my timeline consistent?
- » Are my characters consistent?
- » Are my transitions subtle but clear?
- » Is this section necessary? Can it be cut without affecting the main story?

These and other questions are the ones you ask when story editing. This is the editing that you need most. By the time you finish a manuscript you probably have read every word dozens and dozens of times. See how the story *feels*. If you read a lot, then you should have a feel for a good story or a bad one.

When editing, consider giving your manuscript to a friend or acquaintance to read. But beware. A writer cannot have a soft skin. Take criticism and examine it very carefully. If more than two people say the same thing then maybe there is some truth to it. Pick people who read a lot and who read the type of book that you are attempting to write.

Don't edit yourself too early in the writing process. Some people spend too much time polishing their work and not enough time finishing it. Editing your first couple of chapters over and over can keep you from ever getting to the end. Also, you could end up editing out something that you don't see a purpose for initially but near the end of the book becomes very important. Your subconscious, hopefully, is working for you and planting seeds in your story that you aren't quite aware of yet. If you edit these things out, you lose the possibility of using them later.

A useful technique for story editing is to let the manuscript sit for a while (several days to a week or two) to clear your head and then take another look. Sometimes awkward wording or a story flaw will become clear once you've gained some distance from the work.

REWRITING

Rewriting is a foul but essential word to most writers' ears. Every manuscript I have had accepted for publication needed to be extensively rewritten. Although the original idea stayed the same, something that initially seemed rather vital to the story had to change.

Rewriting is not something that just happens after the first draft is done. It, too, is an ongoing process. Every fifty pages of manuscript, I print the whole thing out and go over it. Every time I change the plot somewhat further on in the manuscript, I have to go back and rewrite everything to fit the change.

It ain't over when you think it's over. When I complete the first draft of a manuscript, my work on that manuscript is somewhere between two-thirds and three-fourths completed. Too many writers are so glad to have finally completed all those pages that the thought of having to go back and rework the whole thing is blasphemous. But it has to be done.

The most important aspect of rewriting is to be honest. You need to objectively look at a piece of work (which you, as the author, know quite intimately) and find the flaws. Most of the time you know when you're writing the flaw that it's a flaw. It's hard to explain this feeling, but trust your gut about what is wrong and needs to be corrected.

Rewriting can vary from having to completely tear apart the manuscript (thank God for computers) to simply making a few changes here and there. But almost every manuscript needs a rewrite.

I suggest you put away a manuscript for a week or two after you finish writing it to allow yourself some mental distance before looking at it again. Give it out for reads and listen to the feedback. However, *don't* make changes simply because someone suggests them if you don't feel they are valid. I spun my wheels on one manuscript making change after change, and what I was changing was the wrong thing. If there is a problem, and you are honest and take your time, you can usually find it better than probably anyone else.

I just received an eleven-page, single-spaced letter of comments from my editor on a manuscript that needs to be rewritten. I know what it feels like to attend a writing retreat and get back a critique that tears the manuscript apart and recommends changes, some of them rather major.

Your first reaction to such a letter is, of course, negative. Take a couple of days to let that feeling pass. Then go through the comments and the manuscript. The next feeling is one close to despair. It appears an almost insurmountable task.

After some more time, you may start realizing there really is a problem and the thought of rewriting will send you into a funk. Finally, you'll accept that, yes, it is a problem but that it can and must be fixed. Then you can begin rewriting.

COPYEDITING

Copyediting is an ongoing process. If you are lucky, your computer will have a spellchecker. I assume you have a reasonable mastery of the written word, so copyediting merely involves putting the time in with a red pencil or pen and paying attention to detail. If you are fortunate enough to be published, you will have professionals go over your work with a fine tooth comb, and even then they will miss a few things.

Remember the following basic rules:

» Don't repeat words or phrases.
» Use a style manual.
» Don't have secret agents. Make sure the reader is clear about your pronoun usage. Always make it clear who is doing what to whom or what.
» The fewer words the better.

A good technique to help eliminate extra words and to make your writing smoother is to read it aloud and have someone with a copy and a red pen listen. Ask her to note where your verbal reading "edits" the copy. You will be surprised how much you change what you have written when you have to speak it aloud.

EDITING TIPS

Remember that verbs are power words. Adjectives and adverbs are weaker words that can dress up your work but can also interfere with the smoothness of the writing. Hemingway is an example of an author who uses verbs as power words and minimizes adjectives and adverbs.

Do not repeat words if you can help it, especially uncommon words, because the second time the reader encounters a redundancy, he'll note it, which interrupts his narrative concentration.

Make sure each adverb you use is essential. Ask yourself if you can eliminate the need for the adverb by choosing a different, stronger, verb.

Avoid overusing verbs that end in -*ing*. The primary purpose of an -*ing* verb is to show simultaneity. For example:

Don was sitting there.
Don sat there.

The second sentence is more direct and smooth.

Avoid vague pronouns. Don't make the reader work to figure out whom you are referring to. Always have an antecedent to your pronoun or it won't make sense. And, of course, omit all unnecessary words.

KILLING IT—THE ULTIMATE EDIT

Numerous aspiring novelists become too enamored of their first manuscript. If you talk to published authors you will find out that the vast majority did not get their first manuscript published. Writing it was an investment in learning. They moved on to write a second, a third, however many it took to get published. It's a difficult thing, but often you have to take the manuscript and shove it in a drawer, give up on getting it published, and move on to writing your next one.

THE READER

You occasionally have to remind yourself that you'll spend months, even years, writing something that others will read and consume in only hours. You also have to remember what the mind-set of the reader is as he approaches your novels. You have to tell a story interesting enough to keep the reader's attention (intellect) and tell it in a manner that makes the reader feel connected to the characters (emotion).

Don't forget what the reader knows. If the reader knows something that a character in your story doesn't, it makes the story harder to write. You have to do this sometimes, but be very careful to not confuse or bore your reader. Don't go ten pages with a character agonizing over who killed Aunt Bess if the reader saw Uncle John strangling Aunt Bess in chapter two, something this character obviously wasn't privy to.

In the same manner, if you have an ensemble cast of characters traveling all over the world, you run into the problem of what we used to call in the army "dissemination of information." The reader knows what all the characters know, but the characters don't know what the other characters know. I used to have scenes where my characters literally all sat around a conference table and exchanged information—at least that is until an editor pointed out to me how boring those scenes were to the reader.

Don't underestimate the reader. If she can read, she has at least a base level education. Most writers err on the side of overkill; although it is just as dangerous to be so subtle the reader misses it. Remember, though, most people read every word and aren't likely to miss what you write. They may miss the significance of what you've written (which is useful in building suspense and having neat twists), but usually when the reader gets to the end and learns what really happened (if it's well written), he suddenly sees the significance of events or dialogue that he didn't pay much attention to earlier. Thus mention Uncle John maybe only once, instead of twenty times. Yeah, he was mentioned and the especially astute reader may pick up your clue, but even the most obtuse will get it if you rant on about Uncle John's massive forearms and great hand strength in chapter ten, and happen to mention several times how he likes to pop the heads off chickens in chapter twelve, and how he used to set fires and torture small animals as a kid in chapter fourteen—get the point?

Overuse of language can be a problem. If a character is upset, you only need to say it once; using very strong adjectives or adverbs further on, in order to emphasize the character's state of mind, can actually detract. Let the actions, not the adjectives and adverbs, speak.

An example of this common mistake:

"Listen you idiot," Buffalo Bill angrily screamed at the quivering boy.
"You've really made me mad now," he furiously added as he pounded the
stock of his rifle into the dead buffalo's already smashed skull.

Think Buffalo Bill is angry? Uh-huh.

Don't lecture the reader. Sometimes you will write something you feel very strongly about emotionally but really adds little to the story. Cutting something can be one of the most painful things to do, but it can also be one of the most necessary. I had a chapter in my second novel that I was very proud of. It was a Special Forces briefback that went into superb detail on the upcoming mission. Unfortunately, it slowed down the action of the book, and I made the decision to cut it down extensively. Chapter six went from thirty pages in the first version to five in the final version. Concentrate on the overall story, not parts of the story.

I've heard people say that you should cut out the part of the manuscript that you absolutely love the most because your emotion is clouding your judgment. I'm not sure I agree with that, but there is a certain degree of validity to taking a hard look at the parts in your story that you feel most strongly about. It might even be just a sentence, or even a word, that strikes you each time you read it, thus taking you out of the story. Be prepared to cut.

Another mistake is too much foreshadowing. I found that I tended to "set up" plot points too much instead of allowing them to occur naturally. Earlier, I discussed Chekov's rule of not having a gun in Act One unless it's fired by the end of Act Three, but be careful not to mention the gun too much or the story loses all suspense.

Remember that to interest your reader, you have to get her involved with your story. Never assume you interest the reader.

In the publishing arc, from writer, to agent, to editor, to publisher, to bookseller, to reader, the reader is the most important component. The reader is the consumer of the product you are inventing and the publisher is producing. Without the consumer, there would be no need for the product.

READ . . . A LOT

My final word on finesse: Read. Read to study style and also for story ideas. Whenever I feel myself start grinding down at the keyboard, I pick up a good book and read. It's a form of inspiration and rejuvenation. I also wander around a bookstore, looking at what has just come out and vowing to myself that I can write better stuff than that. So can you.

→TOOL: 8

YOUR SUBMISSION

BEFORE YOU SUBMIT YOUR NOVEL

You need to do three things *before* you start marketing a manuscript:

1. Make sure you're really finished. You should not start trying to sell a manuscript until it is done. I have seen new writers, with only a partial manuscript and an outline, attempt to approach agents and publishers at conferences. Their feeling seems to be that they will do the work to finish the rest of the manuscript if they find someone interested in it. Unfortunately, that technique doesn't fly in the reality of the business. As I noted earlier, in the majority of cases, writers have several completed manuscripts before they get published.

2. Let the manuscript sit for at least two weeks before making

submissions. Then pick it up, and reread it very critically. Rewrite. Edit. Clean it up. As you read the following pages, the one adjective I repeatedly use with regards to the publishing world is *slow*. No one else is in any rush so you have to fight the urge to spin your wheels. When you send out your submission, you're only going to get one shot at each agent and publishing house; make sure the manuscript is your best one.

3. Start writing your next book. You learned so much writing the first one that your second is bound to be better. Most authors do not get published on their first try out of the gate. To avoid being discouraged, start writing your second book. This prevents you from spending an entire year trying to market the first and ending up with just a pile of rejection slips. At least at the end of the year, at the very least you can have a pile of rejection slips *and* another manuscript ready to sell. I was on manuscript number three with hundreds of rejections on file before I got my first book deal. And I know for a fact that I wouldn't have gotten that book deal if I had not had three manuscripts in hand. Having those extra manuscripts made my first publisher more confident in my commitment. And, with rewriting, these first two did eventually get published.

If you've done those three things, then you are ready to start marketing your book. Think of the ultimate buyer, the reader standing in the bookstore. How does he choose a book? Editors and agents think about that answer quite a bit. So should you.

THE SUBMISSION MIND-SET

The critical components editors and agents are looking for in a novel are good characters revolving around a great idea. Why? Because that is what readers are looking for. Not only does the idea by itself have to be top-notch, but it also has to fit the publisher's needs at the time.

The key to selling your novel is to successfully communicate to the agent or editor the excitement you feel about your book. You started writing an entire novel based on your original idea because it excited you—try to convey that passion to the editor or agent as best you can. You shouldn't "write for the market," but you most definitely need to understand the market when attempting to break into it. Your original idea is the first thing that gets looked at—long before your writing does. Your background (and I mean more than just your writing background) also plays a determining role in how a publisher looks at a submission. Your personal expertise with the subject about which you are writing plays a crucial role.

A common lament among writers is: "If I could only get my manuscript read, I know a publisher would buy it." There is a flaw in the logic of that statement that most people never consider. As I mentioned earlier, how many of you go to a bookstore, completely read a book, and *then* buy it? To expect agents and editors to do that isn't fair. Most readers buy a book from an unknown author based on reading the cover copy and maybe the first couple of pages. Readers use the same criteria as an agent or a publisher.

To an agent or editor, time is money. For them to invest the time to read your manuscript, they have to expect a reasonable return on that investment. And remember, *every* writer thinks her manuscript gives a great return.

Here's a scary thing about the business: When the sales reps for a publisher visit book buyers to get orders for upcoming books, they don't carry boxes full of manuscripts or even bound galleys. They carry cover flats. These are the cover, front and back, spread out flat. On the reverse side is some marketing information about the book and the author. That's it. The sales rep spreads all these flats out on a table in front of the book buyer, like a dealer in poker. They have several minutes to pitch a few of the titles to the buyer. The rest, the buyer browses through briefly to determine how many copies to order.

By the time an average midlist paperback hits the racks, maybe three people in the business have actually read the book. The sales reps certainly don't have time to read them, nor do the buyers for the stores. Scary, isn't it? But it's reality.

THE SUBMISSION PROCESS

At this point your manuscript is done—right?—and ready to market. As you read the following sections, try to follow the methodology I used. First you must find the right publishers or agents to target. Then you must prepare your submission, which may well be the most important piece of work you do to get your writing published. (Note for the purposes of this section, I consider the terms *submission* and *query* to mean the same thing—a submission is also what you will send to agents.) Finding the right places to submit your work and understanding the submission process will greatly increase the chances of your manuscript receiving a good look. The process I describe below will make more sense if you think of it as similar to what a reader goes through when entering a bookstore and perusing a book for purchase.

STEP ONE: FIND THE RIGHT PLACE TO SEND YOUR MANUSCRIPT

In getting started, you must determine who to send your submission to, in the same manner that a reader walks to the part of the bookstore that has the type of books she enjoys reading.

Whenever I look at a book on the shelf, my eye automatically goes to the imprint on the spine that says who the publisher is. If it's a book

THERE IS NO SECRET HANDSHAKE

When I attend writers conferences, I hear the same questions being asked (most of which are answered in this book). The feeling seems to be that some author or, most especially, some editor or agent will suddenly leap to his feet and give the "secret" to getting published.

Another thing I see at conferences are writers getting confused by the different perspectives offered. I watch writers listen to authors all week long. When the editors and agents talk, all the same questions are asked, and the answers from those on the buying end are attended to more carefully than those on the selling end, yet writers are going to be on the selling end. I can tell you how I sell a manuscript—an editor can tell you how she acquires a manuscript. The two are not necessarily equivalent unless you want that specific editor to buy your manuscript. An editor's answers represent her own views and the buying policies of her particular publisher. My perspective is that of an author in the world of publishing, a world that has a variety of places to sell your work.

Some editors and agents spend a lot of time during their conference talks telling the attendees how to make their (the editors and agents) jobs easier. While I don't believe in abusing editors and agents and am a firm believer in being professional, a writer's goal is not to make their jobs easier. It's to work together.

It's important to note the "we-they" attitude between writers and the publishing business. I'm constantly asked how much control I have over cover decisions (very little if any), how much an editor will change the manuscript (always recommendations and almost always for the better of the book), and how publishers will screw over the writer (only if your interests are in opposite directions). Writers, agents, editors, and everyone else at a publishing house are supposed to be on the same team with the same goals. Approach people in the business with a positive attitude, while looking out for your own interests.

similar to what I write, I know that the imprint may be a good publisher to target. Sometimes, the imprint name may be part of a larger house. For example, Spectra is the science fiction imprint for Bantam. To find the publishing house, turn to the copyright page, which will usually have the publisher's address listed. (Another interesting aspect of the copyright page is that you can tell what printing the book is in—there is usually a list of descending numbers. Wherever the numbers stop is number of the printing of that book.)

There are numerous publications such as the annual *Novel & Short Story Writer's Market* and *Writer's Market* that list publishers, and their needs and requirements. These books give both the address and what each one wants in the way of a submission. The information listed also tells you what type of books the individual houses specialize in.

Remember that you do not have to break into the top of the line of the market right from the start. There are numerous smaller presses that are more accessible. Clyde Edgerton has done quite well with Algonquin Books. Contrary to popular belief, I think small presses are making a comeback as a result of corporate mergers.

Lately it seems that fewer and fewer major publishers are accepting unsolicited material and deal only with agents. The submission process I describe in this chapter also goes for submitting to agents, which I will cover in more detail on page 167.

When preparing to market a manuscript, an agent I know says you have to "know the scorecard." You have to know who is who.

Understand also that the corporate takeovers and buyouts have changed the face of publishing. Houses are ferociously eating each other up, and you should know who is who because different imprints in the same house won't always compete against themselves for the same manuscript. Ultimately, this is one of many reasons why you may need an agent.

STEP TWO: PREPARING YOUR SUBMISSION

Whether you send in a query letter or you've already been invited to submit a manuscript, make sure to address your submission to the appropriate editor. Although some publishers will look at unsolicited manuscripts, the majority of entries in *Writer's Market* read like this:

HOW TO CONTACT: Query with outline/synopsis and 2 sample chapters with SASE. Simultaneous submissions OK. Reports in 6 to 8 weeks.

If a publisher does invite unsolicited manuscripts, never send one out unless it's preceded by a query letter (the initial letter sent to an agent or editor intended to raise interest in your novel), and the manuscript has been requested. Many agents and publishers just want a query letter, and if they're still interested, they'll request the synopsis and sample chapters. After that, they may request the manuscript. The danger with this protocol is that it adds an extra step to the process, and every extra step increases the chance of rejection. I highly recommend sending a cover letter, synopsis, sample chapters, and a self-addressed, stamped envelope (SASE).

Before I go into the details of each element, let me give you some general guidelines (and yes, I know you will tell me you have heard different guidelines from Agent So and So, and Editor What's Her Name at that big New York publisher, but what I'm giving you here are the general rules); ignore them at your own risk:

1. All correspondence should be typed. Handwritten material does not fly.
2. Make sure the typing is clear. Use a new ribbon, laser cartridge, whatever. Hard as it is to believe, agents and editors do get

material so faded or poorly printed it is difficult to read. Difficult to read equals a no-go.

3. Use white, 20-pound paper. Do not use erasable bond paper. Your cover letter can be on higher quality paper. Do not use colored paper to try to get attention. You don't want that kind of attention.

4. Use a plain type style. Don't try using weird fonts or graphics. A twelve-point Courier or Geneva font works fine. Use a decent sized font, particularly in your manuscript. I often get manuscript pages on which the font is so small it gets difficult to read. Your font should average out to about 250 words per full manuscript page, give or take 5 percent.

5. There should be no visible corrections on your cover letter.

6. Have 1″ margins all around.

7. The manuscript should be double-spaced (you might be able to get away with a single-spaced synopsis in order to fit it on one page).

8. All material, including sample chapters or the manuscript, should be unbound.

9. Your name or your manuscript's title should be on every piece of paper.

10. Anything longer than one page should be numbered.

The Cover Letter. The first line of your cover letter must grab the reader because it is the first (and maybe the last) line the person opening your material will read. Think of it the same way you think about the inside flap of the book in the bookstore that the reader is looking at.

What is the hook for your manuscript? Why will someone want to buy it? No matter how good your manuscript is, if you don't write a good cover letter, it will never get read. Use your story's original idea as your opening line: "What if. . . ." In this way, you get your reader's attention, and the original idea is planted in his head as he looks through the rest of the submission.

I suggest *not* starting out with the following lines:

» "Enclosed you will find. . . ." Everyone is sending essentially the same thing. The editor or agent expects to find a submission enclosed. When seen fifty times a day, this opening doesn't grab anyone.

» "I've just written my first novel, and I'd like you to take a look at it. . . ."

» "I just know you will love this. . . ."

Go to the bookstore and look at book jackets. Note how they put "*The New York Times* Best-Selling Author" on the cover. Well, since you aren't a best-seller yet, look for the books that have some sort of catchy phrase on the top back, such as the one included on my novel *The Omega Missile*: "A nuclear holocaust is just a button away . . . and someone's about to push it." These types of lines can make good openings for your cover letter. As with any other aspect of writing, however, be careful not to overuse adjectives and praise your own work. Let the facts speak for themselves.

After a paragraph or two on the novel, grabbing the editor's attention and making her drool with anticipation to look at your synopsis, move on. Include not only a sales pitch for the manuscript to the publisher but also a sales pitch for yourself. The manuscript is an extension of you. What special background do you have that would make her want to see what you have done? Along with your writing background, what other story-related background might you want to share? My years in the Special Forces certainly made some editors take a longer look at my cover letter concerning a book about Special

Forces. These paragraphs are your writing résumé. If a publisher accepts your book, she is hiring you. Think about the author bio on the inside back cover of a book. Often people buy books because the author has an interesting background; editors do the same.

This doesn't mean your submission will be ignored if your background doesn't have much direct application to your subject matter and you have little writing experience, but editors and agents also remember what Mark Twain said: "Write what you know." If your job or background in any way applies to what you've written, make sure you mention that.

Unless you've been published in something noteworthy that you've been paid for, don't clutter up the letter with writing credentials. Editors and agents understand you're a new author trying to break through.

While it's good to make a sales pitch in your cover letter, I recommend against marketing the book. What's the difference? The sales pitch consists of you telling the editor what your great idea is. Marketing is telling him who you think will want to read your novel. With fiction, most agents and editors pretty much agree you shouldn't do that for several reasons: (1) Most editors and agents consider themselves the experts on the market; and (2) you will probably be wrong in your estimates. Let the work speak for itself.

Be very, very careful if you try to be humorous. Most of us aren't that funny. I advise staying away from trying to be funny, unless of course, you've written a humorous book, in which case your cover letter better have the agent or editor rolling on the floor. Your cover letter must be one page. No more than that. Sad to say, it's a volume business. An agent I know said he can tell within twenty seconds if a submission is worth considering further.

You may want to add a last sentence giving some factual information about the manuscript such as, "This is an 85,000 word science fiction manuscript."

Make sure you address your cover letter to the editor or agent listed in the submission guidelines. Don't worry about who is really going to look at it. It's better than addressing it to "Hey, you." You may even want to call the publisher to verify the editor still works at that house. Editors tend to move around quite a bit. Also make sure you end your letter with a polite thanks to the editor or agent for her time. Naturally, the letter should be an example of your best writing. Misspellings or poor grammar can hurt you before you're even out of the starting block.

When you think cover letter, think book jacket for a hardcover book. If a publisher likes your letter, she likes your idea. The major purpose of the cover letter is to get the reader to want to read your synopsis. That's it. (For an example of a cover letter, see Appendix B.)

The Synopsis. Again, one page. You will hear other opinions, some ranging up to ten or twenty pages. I say one page simply because I take the editors' and agents' perspective. I don't think you are going to hook them with five pages of synopsis if they don't read past page one. And you may turn them off on page three if they do. Contrary to what we instinctively think, the more someone puts down, the more chance he's going to turn the reader *off* rather than hook the reader. Remember the reader was hooked by your cover letter. A long synopsis might make an interested publisher wiggle off the hook because there's a good chance she'll find something she doesn't like the more she reads. I highly recommend no more than two pages in a synopsis, and I truly think it should be one page.

I just read a four-page synopsis someone sent me to review, and I asked a ton of questions because the more he put in the synopsis, the more questions he inadvertently raised. If he had been more succinct, I would have had fewer questions.

"Oh my God," you say. "How am I going to get four hundred pages of manuscript down to one page?"

It isn't easy. This can take weeks to do, but do it you must. Look at the book jackets for similar books to what you've written. Guess what? They were written in collaboration between published writers and publishers. So be sneaky. Write a book jacket for your book, except tell the entire story. The text for a book jacket is only two or three paragraphs, so you actually have more room than the poor editor does when she tries to prepare copy for a jacket.

In your manuscript, you will have so many important things (*"Everything's* important!" you cry.) that it is bewildering to condense. Try letting someone who has read the book summarize it and see what he comes up with. His distance from the writing might allow him to do it more easily.

The best synopses of my books that I have read were my reviews in *Publishers Weekly*. In those, the reviewer gets the story down to one paragraph. Peruse the magazine and see how a book similar to your own is summarized. You also might want to go to your local bookstore and ask to see some publishers' old catalogues to see how they pitched their books. It could be worthwhile to pitch your book to that publishing house in the same manner.

Although many people feel a one-page synopsis to be unfair, if you look at it from a business perspective, it really isn't. What does a reader do in a bookstore? Look at a book cover, then the jacket or back page to read the less-than-one-page jacket copy. If that doesn't interest her, she doesn't even bother to read the first page, or any other page for that matter. Neither will an editor or agent. Avoid the following mistakes when preparing your synopsis:

1. Too long. Can you go longer than one page? Yes. But every page over, realize that you exponentially increase the odds of losing the reader's interest.

2. Too much detail in certain areas and not enough in others. You always have some great ideas and plot twists that you want to mention. Forget about them. The synopsis is an *overview*.

3. Making the synopsis a list of bullets. First this happens. Then that. Then this. Then that. Did you ever see a book jacket with bullets? The synopsis should be prose.

4. Too many adjectives. "This is an intriguing and fascinating story about a fierce, dedicated, Viking warrior who plunders his rapacious way across Europe told in a scintillating manner, great blah, fantastic blah, blah, blah."

   I can hear the editor's response: "Yes, normally we publish nonintriguing, boring books, but since yours is intriguing and fascinating—because *you* say so in your synopsis—we most certainly want it."

   Just as you have to cut the fat in your book, you have to get rid of the fat in your synopsis. Editors expect good manuscripts to be intriguing, exciting, and captivating. Using those adjectives to describe your own work is a waste of space. Use verbs as your power words, not adjectives and adverbs. Let the work speak for itself.

5. The "What is this story about?" syndrome. There are few things worse than finishing someone's synopsis and still not having a clue what the manuscript is about. Give it to a stranger you meet on the street—or better yet, in a bookstore—and see if he understands it. Have him tell you what he thinks your story is about after reading your synopsis. You might be surprised at the feedback.

6. The "You have eight great stories here in your synopsis but what's the book about?" syndrome. Too often a synopsis turns out to be a muddle of subplots that leaves the reader wondering

what the main story is about. Wondering what—you got it—the original idea is.

7. The "I don't know what kind of story this is? What's the market?" syndrome. I've read a synopsis and then scratched my head wondering if it was a science fiction book, a fantasy, or a children's book? Just where the heck in the bookstore are we supposed to stack this sucker anyway? You are supposed to cover the genre of your book in—you got it—the cover letter (pun intended), but if it's not clear in either the cover letter or the synopsis, it makes the editor or agent wonder if it will be clear when they read the manuscript. If they read it.

8. The "These characters sound very good but what's the story?" versus "This story sounds great but are there any characters in it?" Both are extremes and both are wrong.

9. The "Gee, it sure would have been nice to know your surprise ending, but I don't have the time to respond to your query because you left me hanging," syndrome. Tell the ending. The editor doesn't want to play guessing games, and too often people promise much more than they actually deliver in surprise endings.

10. Psychologists say our short-term memory can hold seven facts. Therefore, I think you shouldn't have more than three names—protagonist, antagonist, and one major supporting character—in your synopsis. Add in the original idea, the hook, the main story line, and the climax, and you've filled the reader's short-term memory. I've read synopses with so many names in them that I can't keep track of anything.

There is another angle to take with a synopsis, particularly if your manuscript does not fit into a specific genre, is more character oriented, or is humorous. A synopsis for such books would not have much of a story, and there would be no hint as to the real uniqueness of the writing. Anne Tyler's *Breathing Lessons*, for example, would make a most boring synopsis because the focus of the story is on strong characters while the plot itself is not particularly exciting.

I mention this because it is important not to sacrifice the uniqueness of your book to try to fit a format. In some cases, the page you use for a synopsis might be better used to give some highlights of the writing. If your book is a series of anecdotes about a family, pick one of the best, make that your "synopsis," and tell the editor this is your book times one hundred.

The major purpose of the synopsis is to get the reader to want to look at your sample chapters. You'll find an example of a synopsis I used for a book in Appendix C.

Sample Chapters. Which ones to send? The first two? The last two? The best two? Remember the purpose of the sample chapters. The synopsis gave the reader the story. The chapters should show the reader how well you write. Some publishers make it easy and tell you to send the first couple of chapters. I advise sending consecutive opening chapters even if the publisher doesn't specify. Consecutive chapters make it easier for the reader to stay with the flow of the story. Sending chapters from the middle or end is too confusing. The major purpose of the sample chapters is to get the reader to want to look at your entire manuscript.

To justify or not to justify? I justify my format, but my computer spaces evenly. Some programs do not space the words evenly on the line and if yours doesn't, then don't justify. Also remember that the title or your name should be on every page as a header, along with a page number, and that chapter breaks should start on a new page.

Self-Addressed Stamped Envelope (SASE). If you want a reply, send an SASE. Isn't it nice that you are paying postage on your own rejections?

If you want the submission itself back, send sufficient postage and a large enough envelope. Otherwise it goes straight in the trash. Major publishers and agents deal with hundreds of submissions each week, and it would get quite expensive if they paid to send it all back. Alternatively you can simply allow it to get thrown out as the cost of postage is usually less than the cost of copying or printing a new submission.

You might send a self-addressed stamped postcard in your packet that agents and editors can use to send back to let you know the packet was received. However, this is only for your sanity. It's not going to make a bit of difference to the people looking at the slush pile.

How quickly will you hear back? From four weeks to never.

What's a reasonable amount of time? Whatever the publisher or editor or agent determines it to be.

What can you do if you haven't heard back in what you consider a reasonable amount of time? Nothing. You have no leverage; you can't make people work faster than they are going to. (Also remember that December and August are dead times in the publishing business, as most people are on vacation.)

What will you get back in your SASE? This will range from nothing, to a "No thanks" written on your cover letter, to a form slip thanking you but declining, to a personalized letter of rejection. If you get the latter (and they are rare), take hope. It means someone took the time and effort to actually reply.

Multiple Submissions. It is all right with publishers if you submit to other publishers at the same time. It takes so long for publishers to reply that you'd be a very old person if you submitted to only one publisher at a time. Don't bother to put on the cover letter that it is a multiple submission. It's a subconsciously negative comment and unnecessary. Don't put anything in your cover letter that doesn't serve a positive purpose.

A WORD OF CAUTION

Having just read this, you are probably raring to write your scintillating cover letter and your sparkling synopsis. But I just finished judging (with some assistance from an agent) a contest on cover letters and synopses, and the first place and second place awards went to people who did not have cover letters in exactly the format I listed above.

"Treachery," you cry. "You have deceived us, you scum-sucking dog," you lament, as I overuse my dialogue tags.

No. I'll tell you why those two entries were chosen. The first place winner had the most intriguing *idea and story*. Keep that in mind. Because you can sculpt a pile of horse manure into a shape that is pleasing to the eye, but it is still horse manure. You have to have substance. The second place person had the most coherently written synopsis along with the second best idea.

The formats I have given throughout this chapter are only guidelines. They do not guarantee success. They may enhance your possibility of success, but ultimately, in order to sell a manuscript, you *must have* two things before even trying a submission: a good idea and smooth writing.

REJECTIONS

Why a whole section devoted to rejections? And right after the section on submissions? Guess what's coming shortly after you start sending out your queries.

THE NEED FOR PATIENCE

In my opinion, the worst thing about being an author is the need for patience. This business is extremely, extremely slow.

I once sent a manuscript to an editor who had asked for it, and I didn't hear back until thirteen months later when I called him. I finally got through. (According to rules editors propagate, you're not supposed to ever, ever call an editor, but a year was my limit.) The editor in question picked up the phone and said: "Editorial."

Having met the editor at a conference earlier, I recognized his voice, but I politely asked to speak to so and so. He told me that so and so (him) was on another line and he (I guess his alter ego) would take a message.

Here I violated one of my rules. I got upset. After all, it had been more than a year since this guy had asked to see my manuscript. He had not answered any of my most polite letters inquiring as to the status of the manuscript. He had not returned any of my recent phone calls. So I called back. When he did the same thing, I told him I recognized his voice and asked him what kind of game he was playing. He got irate and told me that was how he dealt with people calling.

Now, editors certainly have the right to do anything they please. As a writer, you have to decide if you're willing to deal with such people. Unfortunately, in the world of writing, there are a couple dozen writers who get their calls returned and have editors do what they want. The rest of us have to suck it up and drive on.

I also know, though, there are many writers who fail to keep up their end of the professional relationship. Writers who miss deadlines. Who refuse to compromise on editorial work. I exercised my option in this case and sent a polite letter to that editor apologizing for calling and asking him not to review my manuscript.

Nobody is in a rush to do anything. Except you, of course.

Rejection is a fact of life in the writing business and something you *will* face. I have approximately eighty rejections for each of my first two novels. Despite having an agent, my first novel out in hard-cover, and the second and third manuscripts accepted for publication, every publisher soundly rejected my fourth manuscript. Years later, I am reworking that manuscript using all the comments noted in the rejection letters. Another manuscript is gathering dust in my agent's office because we have made a mutual agreement that it is not worth marketing right now and might never be. The publisher who did the first six books in a series rejected me for a seventh book.

The lesson? If you want to be a writer, get used to rejections. It's part of the business.

In fact, the prospect of rejection sometimes keeps writers from sending queries out, which I don't quite understand. If you don't ante up, you can't be in the game.

Ninety-five percent of the time you will get a form letter thanking you for your submission and wishing you luck elsewhere. As I mentioned earlier, if you get a personal letter that means someone really took a hard look at what you sent and was interested. Read carefully any comments made and take them to heart.

It's essential to remember that the publishing business is exactly that: a business. Too many writers approach it from an idealistic perspective. The dollar is the bottom line for the publisher. If they don't see how they can make money off your submission, no matter what its literary qualities, then they won't be interested.

Remember that your novel, once it is completed and submitted, is no longer your "baby" but a product that you have to distance yourself from emotionally in order to survive the ordeal. If you feel bad getting all those form letters, take a peek at *Rotten Rejections*, edited by Andre Bernard, and be glad you aren't getting some of the personalized rejections others did:

» The Bridge Over the River Kwai *(Pierre Boulle). A very bad book.*

» The Good Earth *(Pearl Buck). Regret the American public is not interested in anything on China.*

» The Diary of Anne Frank *(Anne Frank). The girl doesn't, it seems to me, have a special perception or feeling which would lift that book above the "curiosity" level.*

Take heart and hang in there.

NEVER COMPLAIN, NEVER EXPLAIN

You don't get any opportunities to explain your submission when it's sitting on an agent's or editor's desk. So if they don't "get it" the first time around, they won't *get it*. Get it? All your explanations and defenses mean nothing because you not only won't get the chance to say them; you *shouldn't* get the chance to say them.

Learn to control your emotions with rejection. Sometimes you might get a rejection letter back with comments that you totally disagree with or that might be outright incorrect. Don't lash out. There are people running this business. You won't agree with some things, particularly rejections, but do not complain, write nasty letters, make obnoxious phone calls, or send dirty faxes. You never know when you are going to run into those people again.

My first book was published by a publisher who had rejected my query for that same book. I had disagreed strongly with some of the points in that first rejection letter, still do as a matter of fact, but I ate it and drove on. If I had sent a nasty letter, methinks they would have remembered me and not even considered the manuscript when my agent submitted it.

Agent Richard Curtis's first piece of advice to writers in his book

Beyond the Bestseller consists of a few simple words: "Keep your big mouth shut."

The longer I have been doing this for a living, the more I realize the profundity of those words. If an action you plan to take, words you plan to utter, a letter you want to write, an e-mail you want to send, could have anything other than a positive reflection back on you, *don't do it.* Acting out of anger, frustration, or righteous indignation will bite you in the butt, to put it mildly.

It is hard sometimes not to react. In many aspects, publishing is a very poorly run business. And those bad business decisions in New York can adversely affect you. They can destroy you in some cases. But you have to drive on and you have to accept that you, by yourself, are not going to change the entire publishing industry.

MAKING THE BEST OF REJECTION

For each acceptance I have (thirty-two now), I have at least twenty to thirty rejections on average. I also get rejected for teaching jobs at seminars, magazine articles I submit, and movie options. It's part of the business, and you have to use it to your advantage. Take strength from any positive comment. And also remember that you don't know how and when your break will come—perseverance counts, but you are also dealing with people and courtesy counts also.

Many times the rejection has nothing at all to do with the work itself. Sometimes a publishing house has no room at the inn. Their list is full for the next couple of years, and they simply can't buy any more material for a while. Sometimes they don't see how they can market a particular book even though they think the idea is great and the writing fine. Even if you have an excellent idea and manuscript, you might be rejected simply because the publisher already has a similar manuscript programmed into the production schedule. Sometimes editors may like a work but the publisher or the sales force see a problem, whether it be not being able to market the title or not getting booksellers excited about the type of novel.

One frustrating aspect of rejections is the second read. The first editor likes your work, but he needs a second opinion. So he asks a second editor to look at the manuscript. The second editor may not like your manuscript.

The best advice I received regarding rejection came from an agent at Creative Artists Agency (CAA) when I asked him about a manuscript that had been rejected by a bunch of studios. He told me that a rejection is an emotional decision. The person who made the rejection goes back and invents reasons for that decision, sometimes correctly, but many times incorrectly.

One aspect of rejections I find fascinating is the "We want something like X, but not like X," reaction. I got a rejection back from a studio considering my novel *Area 51* that said, "This book is too much like *Independence Day*, and no one wants to be compared to the fourth highest grossing movie of all time." You have to really sit and think about what that sentence says. My reaction is, "Hell yeah, I want to be compared to such a success."

There's no way around this mind-set. In many ways, Hollywood and the New York publishing world have "group-think." Either everyone wants something or no one wants it. They constantly say they want something different and daring, but they'll reject something because it's different and daring.

Rejections are a subjective process.

I recently cut out a newspaper article on a woman who finally had a manuscript accepted. It's her *thirty-third* manuscript—none of the previous ones were accepted. That's dedication.

Rejection can be good if you learn from it and are able to read between the lines. I received a rejection on a new manuscript from an editor who had previously bought manuscripts from me at another publishing house. His only specific comment was, "I like Bob's work and have bought it before, but this is the same as what he did then."

What I took from that was that I had to get better. I couldn't keep doing the same thing and expect to move up.

If you do happen to get a nasty rejection where someone makes insensitive comments, console yourself with the thought that you wouldn't want to work with agents or editors who would do such a thing. Remember, if they do it to you, they do it to other people, and that is not a formula for success in any business.

You have to have a thick skin as a writer. It's guaranteed, even if you get published, that someone, somewhere, will not like your book, and that at least one of those people will make it her life's mission to inform you.

THE AGENT

The agent is a key player in the publishing business. If there were no agents, publishing houses would have to hire more people to wade through their slush pile. There are very few major publishing houses that will even look at material if it isn't submitted through an agent. It's simply a question of economics. The agent is the link between the author and the publishing world. Having an agent can be the most critical for new writers with no background in publishing. It *is* a jungle out there, and your agent should be your guide. The agent should know who, where, what, how much, and when.

WHAT AGENTS DO

Agents know the market both in terms of what's selling and who's buying. They also know which houses do which stories and can direct your manuscript not only to the correct publishers, but also to the correct editors at those publishing houses. They are on top of the latest changes in the publishing industry and should know what the current needs are.

In most contracts, an agent will be the sole source for all literary properties produced by you except if he chooses not to take on a work. It then reverts back to you.

Some agents are ex-editors so they have an idea how to make a manuscript marketable. Others spent years working in agencies learning their trade. I was under the mistaken impression that my agent would go through my work with a fine-tooth comb, looking over every page carefully. That rarely happens. Again, remember it's a volume business. The same is true of editors to a certain extent. If your manuscript is not basically acceptable in its present form, you won't get a contract. On my first manuscript, my agent faxed me a page of suggestions. I made the suggested changes, and we eventually sold the manuscript. Ever since then, the agents I've worked with generally tell me in a letter or phone call what their suggestions and problems are with a manuscript, and it's up to me to make the corrections.

If your manuscript is right on the margin of being publishable, it is much more likely that an agent will work with you to make it marketable than an editor will. Editors work with authors under contract, and they screen submissions. They very rarely work with something to bring it up to snuff so that it can be brought to contract.

Agents negotiate sale or lease of rights to works, including translation. This includes sales to foreign markets. Normally agents charge a higher percentage fee for foreign rights because they have to split the fee with a foreign agent. Most agents have contacts with various foreign representatives and with a Hollywood agent for film rights.

An agent reviews and negotiates contracts. For a new writer who has no idea what the market is like, this is very important. Contracts vary from publisher to publisher, and I've seen some terrible ones writers ended up signing. I'll often hear writers say they'll get a lawyer to review a contract if it comes to that point. But unless he is an entertainment lawyer, he won't understand the standards of the business. Besides, entertainment lawyers live in Hollywood and deal with movie people, not books.

Agents collect monies due and render shares. This can be very frustrating for both the author and agent, but having the agent do it at least allows the author to maintain a semblance of cordiality with his publisher. My rule of thumb is that my agent takes care of all business contacts with my publisher. Once a contract is negotiated, I generally work directly with my editor on the written work unless there is a large difference of opinion.

Agents examine royalty statements (as if anyone could make sense of them to start with). They also check on the publisher's performance and how they handle your manuscript. Just because you are getting published doesn't necessarily mean you are going to make any money beyond the advance. The agent can help you track what the publisher plans on doing with your book, particularly in such important areas as selling the subrights, designing the cover, and planning for publicity.

Don't expect any paychecks in the mail quickly. Agent Richard Curtis has a running bet with publishers that a writer can write a book faster than the publishers can cut a check. You may laugh, but I have literally done that—written an entire manuscript while waiting for a contract to be drawn up and a check cut.

Like any other business, you have to stay on top of your agent. You are the ultimate protector of your interests. A good agent will advise you, but it should always be your decision as to what actions to take regarding you and your property.

Remember that the agent ultimately works for himself, not you. Remember too that the publishers cut the checks, which go to the agent, who takes his share and then renders the author her share. So if things start getting sticky between you and your publisher, your agent might not put his neck totally on the line to protect your interests. He has other authors who work with that same publisher, and he will want to maintain his relationship with the publisher, perhaps to the detriment of your relationship, although this is rare. Ultimately, agents' loyalties lie with their writers rather than the publisher. Also, of course, remember that the reverse is true—your agent holds some power with the editor because the agent might or might not steer future good work toward that editor in the future.

Some agents require contracts that stipulate what the roles are, what she will do, and what you are required to do. You should work with an agent on a case-by-case basis. Your agent should have the first chance to look at what you produce. She then should let you know whether she wants to work with you on the manuscript or not. If she doesn't, you are free to do whatever you like with it. This is important because you don't want someone representing you simply because you have a contract, especially if she isn't enthusiastic about a particular manuscript.

It can be just as likely that it is the *author's* fault for a bad relationship with an agent as the reverse. I often hear authors complain bitterly about agents. I take such comments with a grain of salt because ultimately the person who produces the product is the author, not the agent. If the product is not good, it does not matter how good the agent is. Very rarely will you find an author willing to admit that maybe his writing didn't measure up.

HOW TO FIND AN AGENT

Most writers hate the quandary that searching for agents put them in. The catch-22: You need an agent to get published, but you can't get an agent unless you're published.

That's not really true. Agents are constantly on the lookout for

new writers; that's how they stay in business. There are several ways
to find an agent:

1. You can do direct submissions using those agents listed in
books such as the annual *Writer's Market* (or WritersMarket
.com). Just like publishers, thousands of agents list their wants
and submission guidelines.

2. Get a recommendation from a published author. The key word
there is *recommendation*. I've had total strangers call me up and
ask for the name of my agent or editor. Then a few proceed—
without asking me—to use my name in a submission saying I
recommended them. Besides being impolite, it really doesn't
help. Some people put so much effort (I know because *I* did)
into simply trying to get their work seen, that they overlook
the fact that even if it is seen, it might not be worth the look.
As I've mentioned in other places, you only have one shot with
each person you submit a piece of work to. Make damn sure
it's your best shot.

3. A book editor that you make a direct submission to might
recommend an agent. Remember above where I talked about
the role of the agent? An editor who feels your work has some
merit but is not quite up to the standard that merits a contract
might suggest an agent you can work with to improve the work.
Contrary to popular myth, not all editors enjoy rejecting manuscripts. Most of them actually do want to see writers succeed.
I should know. I found one of my agents through an editor
who gained nothing at all from the deal. (He worked for a
nonfiction publisher that, in my desperation, I had sent my
fiction proposal to, which by the way violates the advice an
agent gave out at a conference I attended.)

4. Instructors at writing seminars can be a good source but, like

I mentioned above, it works both ways. You should have something that makes them think it's worth their agent's time.

5. Teachers in MFA programs usually have contacts. This is an old boy network that takes care of its own. If that's the route you choose, make the best of it.

6. Some agents advertise through Web sites. Online can be a relatively cheap way to network.

Like most publishers, most agents automatically reject unsolicited manuscripts. The majority of legitimate agents will look at cold submissions received through the mail (such submissions are commonly referred to as "slush"). I do *not* recommend cold phone calls or faxing submissions. If you come off as an irritating person during your contact with the agent, it might not matter how good your manuscript is. The agent simply might not want to work with you. I heard a prominent agent tell of letting go of one of his authors because the author bypassed him and was very rude to some of the people at a publishing house.

FEE-CHARGING AGENTS

In many listings, agents are broken down into two categories: those who charge a reading fee, and those who don't. You can get varying opinions as to the pros and cons of going to an agent who charges a reading fee. Look at the reality of what you want: Do you want to get published, or do you want feedback on your work? If you want to get published, go to those who don't charge a fee.

Some fee-charging agents make their money reviewing manuscripts—not selling them to publishers. My opinion is don't go with such an agent. First, try submitting to those who don't charge. If they all come back negative, and you get no decent feedback, it's your money.

In many cases, it's not necessary to get all four hundred pages of your manuscript reviewed. If you are paying by the page, send a submission (cover letter, one-page synopsis, and the first couple of chapters) and see what the agent has to say before sending the whole thing. Make sure you get feedback not only on your manuscript but also on the synopsis and cover letter.

Also try going to writers' conferences and asking around. Sooner or later you will run into someone who has submitted to a fee-charging agent, and you will get some feedback as to not only the whole process, but also about specific agents.

How would I operate if I ran an agency that charged a fee for reading submissions? One advantage: I could hire extra people to go through a larger volume of submissions in more detail, searching for those that are deemed publishable. (That is also an advantage to you, the writer.) Another advantage would be that I might be able to work

HOW CAN YOU TELL IF AN AGENT IS LEGITIMATE?

When looking for an agent, use common sense. Think of the person who offers to sell you the Brooklyn Bridge. If an agent promises you he will sell your work, I wouldn't believe him. No agent can make that promise unless he has some sort of kickback deal going with a vanity press.

A legitimate agent should be willing to tell you who some of his clients are and even refer you to one if he wants you to sign with him. An agent also should have a track record of sales to legitimate publishers that he can refer you to.

Remember, though, there is a pecking order to agents. As a new writer, you might not be able to get the number one guy or gal in town. You might hook up with someone who is starting out and has few clients and sales to her name.

with someone who is marginal (given that he's paying me some bucks, that is), whereas I wouldn't be able to if my time was my money.

A disadvantage: I would tend to focus a lot more energy on making money out of the volume of submissions received and spend a lot of time on unpublishable material (a disadvantage to you, the writer). I would also appear to put a lot of time and effort into each submission, but in reality I could work off a computer boilerplate of common mistakes and simply go through, make a few changes in the boilerplate, and send you back thirty pages of an apparently in-depth review, which would actually be the same as buying a writing book except a lot more expensive.

I'm not saying that all fee-charging agents do either good or bad. Just remember, it's your money.

SWITCHING AGENTS

Sooner or later, almost every published writer thinks about switching agents. This might happen if:

1. You are going nowhere with the agent you have. No sales.
2. The agent recommends you go elsewhere.
3. You feel like your work is improving but your current agent keeps marketing it at the same level you've been at. Publishing is an up or out business, so this doesn't do you much good.
4. You are changing genres, and your current agent doesn't like or adequately represent your new genre.
5. You want to move up. There are levels to agents just as there are levels to editors. Certain agents can place a manuscript at a certain level in a publishing house. Others can go right to the top.
6. Your agent's main concern is selling your next book rather than establishing your long-term career. The two are not necessarily synonymous.

Ultimately, you should feel good after talking to your agent, not bad. You should feel like the agent is representing you in the best possible and *realistic* light. You should feel that your agent views your career as an upward ride.

For more writers, though, it's a good thing just to get an agent to represent you at all. Remember that agents are businesspeople and are not there to hold your hand or keep you together psychologically while you write (unless of course you write best sellers). Also remember that you are not the only client an agent has.

If you want to sell to a small press, you should know that they usually don't pay an advance and rarely deal with agents. Agents rarely deal with them. When you are doing your submissions, you most likely will query both publishers and agents.

If you go to a conference and have to choose between talking to an agent or an editor, choose the agent. The agent has multiple outlets for your work, while the editor only has one.

Agents are a reality of the publishing business that you need to understand and work with.

AGENTS AND MULTIPLE SUBMISSIONS

As I've said before, the keyword in publishing is *slow*. Agents respond quicker than publishers do, but you could still grow very old waiting. Most agents will only read your manuscript if they have it exclusively. Here's my suggestion:

Do send a query to the number one agent on the list you made from the sources above. Wait a week, and then send to the number two agent. Week three, agent three. Don't tell them it's a multiple query. If an agent calls to ask for the manuscript, she will ask you if anyone else has seen the manuscript. Answer honestly. Send the manuscript. Then hold on your submissions to other agents.

What if *another* agent you queried calls and wants to see the manuscript? My reply: You should be so lucky. But, in the one in a thousand chance you are, tell him it is with the other agent and that you will contact him as soon as you hear back from agent number one. This doesn't necessarily hurt your chances with agent number two, because it actually confirms his interest. Don't try to leverage agent one with agent two. Have patience, take some sedatives, and wait. Well, don't just wait. Be writing that next manuscript.

→TOOL: 9

YOUR BUSINESS

THE PUBLISHING PROCESS

Why do you need to understand the business end of novel writing? Because being an author is being self-employed in the world of publishing. The more you know about the business, the more success you will have.

I can already see legions of literature graduate students holding up their collected works of Faulkner and Shakespeare, but hey, Faulkner meandered out to Hollywood in 1932 to make a buck, and Shakespeare didn't let them do his plays for free. If Faulkner had never been paid for what he wrote, he might have spent the rest of his days in the post office in Oxford.

It is critical that authors understand the perspective of all the other players in the business: editors, agents, publishers, book buyers, bookstore owners, reviewers, anyone who has anything to do with the life of a book (including as mentioned earlier, the reader). Too often, authors get on a high horse and decry all those other players in the business, but in doing so they tend to cut their own throats. Some authors feel that without writers, there would be no book industry. (Watch the scene in *The Player* where they discuss how great the movie business would be if they could only do away with the writers.)

It is true that without writers there would be no publishers, but without any of those other people in the business, there wouldn't be any books. None of those people may have your interests as their number one priority, but they also don't have screwing you, the author, on their priority list either. For many, making money is a priority, but most agents, editors, publishers, and book buyers are in the business because they love books. Like me, they probably could make a better living doing something else, but they're in it because they want to work around books.

I've had people in publishing make moves and do things that were not advantageous to me, but if I were in their shoes I probably would have done the same things they did because it was advantageous to them. If you understand that, you will have more control of your destiny or, at the very least, not as many stomach problems.

Most of the other people in the business actually enjoy getting manuscripts published, even though it might not seem that way to you as the rejection slips pile up. Why else would they be doing what they are doing? Editors and agents love to find that rare diamond that they can publish, but they have to sift through at least ninety-nine submissions to find one worthy of taking a look at.

The business end is extremely important but I issue one caveat here: Just as I recommend not getting so caught up in the actual writing world that you ignore the business end, don't do the opposite. Knowing everything there is to know about the business end of publishing won't get you published if you don't have a well-written and thought-out manuscript based on an excellent idea. I've run into some people who are so concerned about getting to know this person and that person in the business, getting their manuscript looked at, or going to conferences and getting interviews, that they forget to take an honest look at the manuscript. They fail to realize it is poorly written or that the original idea of their story is simply not that innovative or appealing.

There is a very thin line between aggressively marketing yourself and your work and being obnoxious. Writers fall on the obnoxious side when their manuscripts are not worthy of publication. They fall on the aggressive side when their manuscripts are. Of course, that doesn't help you much. My suggestion is to watch the reactions of those you deal with. If five consecutive people, whether they be agents, editors, or other authors, shy away from you after looking at your work, take the hint and take a harder look at what you have rather than trying to hunt down more people to look at it.

Remember: Act professionally even though you might not be treated in the same manner in return. Always take your time and carefully understand a situation before acting. Look out for your interests in every interaction.

FROM MANUSCRIPT TO PUBLISHED BOOK

It all starts with the submission. So let's discuss how submissions are handled. There are two types: cold submissions and requested submissions.

The first is your brown envelope in the mail to the publishing house you looked up in *Writer's Market*. No one at the publishing house specifically asked for you to send your query. That makes it a cold one.

The trend nowadays in the major houses is to not even deal with cold submissions, which makes the role of the agent a growing one.

But since almost all the smaller houses, and some of the major ones, still do, let's discuss the life of the slush pile. As with the rest of publishing, the operative word is *slow*. Some of the big publishers get hundreds of queries a day. They have very low-paid people wading through the pile. Sometimes, smaller houses will have "parties" every couple of months where they stay late several nights and attack the slush pile, which helps explain why you haven't heard from them in three months. It also explains the coffee and donut stains on the rejection notes.

Think of the attitude of the person who has to deal with those stacks of envelopes. Think of the state of her brain. Imagine yourself, sifting through page after page of, on the average, very bad ideas that are presented very poorly. I don't say that to be mean, I actually say that inspire you—after all, *your* query is exciting, professionally done, and well written, right? Those people actually are yearning to see something exciting and good, so give it to them.

You will spend many months waiting for replies from publishers. Some will never reply. One lucky day you might get that most happy of news: Send in the entire manuscript to be read. Then the waiting game starts anew. Months drag by. Then, maybe, just maybe, you'll get an offer. Often you will be referred to an agent as we discussed in the last chapter.

The other type of submission is the requested one. This usually happens when an agent submits your work to a publisher. You have already gone through the weeding-out process of the query and the manuscript review at the agent level. The agent works with you on the manuscript and gets it to a level where he thinks it is marketable. He will come back to you with ideas about where and how to send your work. He may say: "I think you have a midlist mass-market paperback. I'd like to show it to the following five publishers."

You may retort, "Why, no, I think I have an original hardcover best seller." In which case you have a problem between you and your agent. It has taken me almost a dozen manuscripts on the market to get a feel for both my work and the market, and even then I still don't really know what's going on at the publishers' end, so I have to trust my agent. As a new writer, you aren't in a very good position to judge what is going on either. I'm not saying roll over and play dead, but be realistic.

After you and the agent decide how and where to market the book, the agent makes copies of the manuscript and mails them out to the editors he has already talked to about the manuscript. Note this interesting part of the process: Your agent makes a "query" for your manuscript to the publisher over the phone or over lunch. Your agent says, "Well, Ellen, I've got this very good thriller manuscript about _____ . I think it will work as _____ ." Your agent has to describe your work in a couple of sentences and place it in the market, usually by genre.

Yet another reason why I am very big on that original idea and genre: I've had my agent call up and say, "Tell me about the book in a sentence or two." I know that what he is going to do is turn around, call an editor, repeat that same sentence or two, and ask if he can send in the manuscript.

What is good for you in this situation is that manuscripts placed by agents get read much more quickly. And you will get back a signed rejection letter if it isn't bought.

THE CONTRACT

A typical publisher's contract will include at least the following:

» Delivery of an *acceptable* manuscript by a certain date.
» Corrections after acceptance cannot exceed 10 percent or you are charged for composition.
» Who has rights. If you are going with a hardcover publisher,

that publisher will usually control the paperback rights (along with 50 percent of the royalties).

» Who retains dramatic adaptations rights, e.g., film (usually, it's the author).

» The amount of the advance and when it will be paid. Usually the advance is broken down into three payments. The first portion comes at contract signing. The second at acceptance of the manuscript and the third sometime after (it may be when half the manuscript is delivered or at time of publication).

» Royalties and how often they will be paid (usually twice a year). Royalties are interesting because they are accounted twice a year, usually at the end of June and December. Then the publisher takes three to four months to issue a statement. Frustrating, but again, not much you can do about it.

» Author's copies (usually ten).

» Protection of work (copyright, infringement).

» Numerous other details such as audio rights, electronic media rights, etc.

If you are representing yourself, contact the Authors Guild (see Appendix D), and, for a small fee, they will send you a full-length suggested contract for reference. You can compare it to any offer you get. The problem is that authors don't seem to have much power (unless you are on the very top of the pile like Stephen King). In publishing, there's not much of a middle class among authors. There is a handful of elite, and then there is everyone else, scrambling at the bottom in the pack.

The most critical word in your contract is *acceptable*. When does a publisher accept a work? Your guess is as good as mine. Horror stories abound of writers cranking out a manuscript under contract, sending it to a publisher who says, "Yeah, it's okay," and then getting a phone call months later saying, "Your manuscript is not acceptable, and we want our advance money back." Joan Collins had a very bad experience with just this clause and had to sue her publisher. And she won.

It would be nice, and you can try, to get a better definition of the term. Of more practicality, try to at least get a time line on how long a publisher can sit on a manuscript before giving you a decision on acceptability.

THE PUBLISHING TIMELINE

The following is a typical timeline from the moment you sign that wonderful contract through actual arrival of the book in the bookstore. Pay close attention to the number of months that pass—there's a quiz at the end.

Month 1: Sign contract (usually about two to three months after the publisher agrees to terms over the phone).

Month 4: The editorial process begins. The amount of time this takes depends on how much revision the manuscript requires. It is important for new writers to know that publishers won't buy a manuscript if it requires extensive revisions. New writers who think they have a spectacular and novel (no pun intended) idea that with some editorial assistance will become a best seller are setting themselves up for disappointment. If the manuscript isn't pretty much already in a publishable form, it won't be bought.

The editorial process tends to get longer the more books an author has published. While that sounds contradictory, think about it for a second. It takes longer for those novels contracted in the concept stage than it does for those contracted as completed manuscripts. With the latter, the publisher has pretty much accepted the manuscript. With the former, the publisher has accepted the concept; when the first draft of the manuscript is delivered, there is more of a tendency from the publisher and editor to change things.

The first stage of the editorial process is when the editor presents a report to the author. This usually happens a month or two (or more depending on the production schedule) after she receives the manuscript. The manuscript has received a couple of readings by an editor who then passes on her thoughts. Her notes could consist of changing the ending, adding more twists to the plot, deepening characters, etc. The author makes the suggested changes (or argues them, but usually

MULTIPLE BOOK CONTRACTS

Publishers are investing in your name when they publish your manuscript. Because of that, they tend to want more than a one-shot deal. Initially that sounds great—you get to sign two or three book contracts right from the get-go. The disadvantage, though, is that you lock yourself into that publisher at a price range that may not be your true worth two or three years down the line.

Unfortunately, most writers who are scrambling around in the pack don't have too much choice in this area—you need the advance money in order to continue writing. Just be aware, though, that there are disadvantages to signing several book contracts at the same time.

One such disadvantage is called "joint accounting." That's where the publisher ties both your advances together for two books. Even if your first one earns out its advance, you don't see royalties until you earn out the advances for both, even though the second one hasn't been published yet.

The big advantage of multiple book contracts, though, is that you are employed. You can write a book that has already been contracted for publication.

bows to the inevitable—after all, it is the publisher who makes the final determination of "acceptability"). Then the manuscript is sent back for final approval of story. After that, the editor sends it to a copy editor who does the final polishing—checking grammar, punctuation, and spelling.

Then the author gets the manuscript back for final changes. It has already been through a copyeditor, so the writer should have very minor changes. The 10 percent change rule applies here.

The edited manuscript is then sent to production, which is a group of several small elves who stand around and cast spells over the pages. No, actually, production is where the manuscript is designed and type-set. Nowadays, they usually use computer disks or scanning to prepare the pages. The page proofs are printed and the author may receive loose galley proofs. These are 8½" by 11" pages showing what the actual book pages will look like. You proofread these and send them back. At this point, the front matter (title page, table of contents, dedication, and copyright page) is completed.

At the same time the elves in production are working on the book, the dwarves over in marketing are designing the cover, and developing copy and promotional material, which for a new author consists of "Hey, here's a new book."

You may then receive bound galley proofs. These are the same as the loose galleys (with the same mistakes—corrections are made later), only they're bound with cardboard covers. These galleys are sent to reviewers for advance review and to book buyers for their orders (these numbers that will help your publisher determine how many copies of your book will be printed).

Around fifteen months after signing the contract you get a look at a copy of your book's cover. It's too late to change anything, so you love it. The actual printing takes about six to eight weeks.

Month 18: Your book is published.

From a publisher's point of view, here is the timeline. Let's use a manuscript delivery date of January 1 and a publication date of September.

January:

» Minor or major editorial changes made.

» Publication month scheduled. (Note that for publishers September to November is the most dangerous time to schedule a book because it is the most crowded. You're competing with the big boys and girls.)

» Initiate cover design ideas.

February:

» Copy editing.

» First sketches on cover presented.

» Jacket copy prepared.

» Fact sheet/book brief created, used internally.

» Design pages (font, graphic elements, etc.).

March:

» Pre-sales (launch) meeting. Selling the book to the rest of the house, which of course has no time to read the vast majority of books it's selling.

» Publicity planning.

» Co-op advertising considered (the amount of money spent with booksellers for special placement on promotional tables, etc.).

» Set price.

» Book is positioned in the market.

» Editor prepares the catalogue copy.

April:

- » First pass through the galleys.
- » Bound galleys are sent to reviewers.
- » Marketing budget set.
- » Press kit prepared.
- » Fall catalogue released.

May:

- » Sales reps given sales kits, which include information about the book.
- » BEA, the old ABA convention, occurs. Publishers present their titles to the rest of the publishing community.

June:

- » Orders come in.
- » Publication date confirmed.

July:

- » The book is actually printed.

August:

- » The book arrives at the warehouse.
- » Book is shipped.
- » The book is in the store by the last week of the month.

September:

- » The publication (pub) date.

So, how many months from signing the contract to the bookstore? Add in the time it takes you from original idea to finished manuscript. How long does that come to? One year? Two years? Go way back to where I wrote about your story idea. Factor in, say, at least a two and a half years, most likely three. What that means is if you are writing about a subject that may change in the next three years, you'd better be careful. In 1988, one of my manuscripts featured the Russian bogeyman as the enemy. Well, in 1988 this was valid. In 1989 the Wall came down. Oops. A word to the wise: Be careful with time-sensitive stories.

THE PUBLISHING COMPANY AND YOUR EDITOR

When you get your first contract offer, you will probably be so excited you'll sign anything. Having an agent will help, but even that's no guarantee the contract is a good one. I bring this up because, sad to say, writers as a rule are not treated very well by publishers. Not because publishers are mean, but because they usually don't have to treat writers well. There is no union, and your only rights are the ones in the contract, and even then, you need an expert to point them out to you. This is not to say publishers are evil (although many writers I've met think that way). Publishers are simply doing exactly what you or I would be doing—looking out for their own interest. So you do the same—look out for your own interests.

I pay very close attention now to my contracts, but even then, there is only so much leeway a publisher will give you. As I mentioned earlier, the Authors Guild, Inc. will send you a copy of a recommended trade book contract for a small charge. Unfortunately, large publishing houses have a boilerplate contract that they offer, and the moon and the stars would have to be in very strange alignment for them to change it for you, new author. Again, even with a contract, publishers will look out for their own interests first and yours secondly. Remember also that your agent may have other authors whom he represents to that same publisher. Thus your agent may be leery of standing up for you if it means making an enemy of that publisher. On the other hand, the publisher might not want to alienate your agent or you.

You have to understand what your publisher is doing and how he makes money. If you are being published in hardcover and the house doesn't do paperback, the publisher is going to make money by selling subrights to your novel to a paperback publisher (hopefully) and foreign rights to a foreign publisher.

Your editor is usually your "voice" at the publishing house. But be aware that editors move between houses. When your voice is gone, your manuscript has also lost its voice. Additionally, your editor is not the only voice at the publisher and certainly not the last voice. Remember that your editor works for the publisher, not you. Every editor I started working with at each publisher was not the editor I finished working with. Fortunately for me, my works were still published, but it is a common horror story that when an editor leaves, those works that that editor acquired might be canceled.

A large problem in the publishing business is simply geography. It is very rare that an author lives in the same town as her publisher. While you may have visions of being flown to New York to discuss your work over lunch in downtown Manhattan, I recommend you be thankful you get your ten free copies when the work is published.

When I teach, I tell the story of the first glimpse I had of a copy of my second novel, *Dragon Sim-13*. I was at Fort Bragg on active duty (I'd anxiously waited weeks for my copies to arrive via UPS, but by the time I had to leave, they weren't there). So there I was at Bragg when I met another fellow from New Jersey. He looked at my nametag quizzically. He said my name sounded familiar, and he asked me what I did. I told him I was a writer and the cloud on his face cleared up. He reached into his backpack and pulled out a copy of my second novel, which his wife had gotten out of the library for him to read on the plane. The lesson I learned from all that is that New Jersey has a very efficient public library system. No, actually, it was another of many lessons I've learned about patience.

You will most likely not meet anyone at your publisher for several years unless you live close by and make the effort to visit or arrange to go to the same conference. You will also rarely meet your agent unless your travel arrangements happen to coincide. Dealing with people exclusively over the phone and in letters is very difficult and requires some care and consideration. It takes time to get a good feel for someone under such circumstances.

At my ten-year point in the business, with thirteen books published and five more under contract, I had met my first agent once face to face. That was it. I used to say those words with pride, but in reality that was a big mistake on my part. In 2002, I drove up to New York City after arranging meetings with my editors and an interview with a new agent I was considering signing with (having already let go of my second agent). I should have done it five years before that. I think face-to-face meetings are important for both sides to get to know each other. Also, there are things you can ask and discuss in person that are difficult over the phone, or via mail or e-mail.

REVIEWS

I used to say any review is a good review. I say that because a review gives your novel exposure. Most reviews consist of a brief summary of the plot and then a few lines with the reviewer's comments. Be glad that your book has been summarized for you and exposed to readers. Accept that the reviewer's comments have been written and there is nothing you can do about it.

However, there is no doubt that bad reviews can hurt, not only in terms of ego, but also in terms of sales. When you write for a living, the product of your work is out there for anyone to look at and comment upon. The decision by online bookstores to allow people to post an anonymous review of any book for all the world to see is a curious phenomenon, and one many writers are fighting. It's guaranteed that someone will not like your book.

For many writers, once a book has been published it is no longer as important to them. As I discussed earlier, by the time a book is published, the writing of that particular title is years ago, and you are presently working on something that is several manuscripts removed. Such distance can help you not get as hurt by a negative review.

For example, by the time my third manuscript, *Cut-Out*, was released in print, I was working on my ninth. I could hardly remember the entire plot of the third. I certainly felt my writing skills were somewhat better, thus being hit up again for weak characterization didn't hurt as much—indeed, it gave me a focal point to work on when improving my writing skills. Pay attention to responsible reviews. Take what is said seriously, and use it as a learning point. If you get a negative reaction, consider it a compliment that someone cared enough to get really angry or upset about what you wrote; at least I reached them on some level. It's better than apathy.

PEOPLE IN THE BUSINESS

Editors and others in the trade work their way up by playing musical chairs. They step up the ladder by moving to higher positions at other publishing houses.

At one publishing house, I have been through five different editors in the course of five years and five books published. I've also been through five different publicists in the same period of time.

There is an advantage to such jumping though. It means you now know an editor at a house that hasn't published you. It gives you a window to market a new manuscript.

You have to do some work yourself to get reviewed. Your publisher will hit the usual places (*Kirkus Reviews*, *Publishers Weekly*), but it's up to you to find other avenues of exposure, such as alumni newsletters, trade magazines, and local papers.

You have to target venues for reviews. There are magazines out there for every conceivable subject matter. Dig out the ones that relate to the subject matter of your book. Be prepared to purchase copies of your book from your publisher in order to send review copies out.

NUMBERS AND THE ENTERTAINMENT BUSINESS

Publishing is a business. I was part of it for ten years before I really understood what I was part of: the entertainment business. That's a term that most people don't stop to examine. But in the same way the term *military intelligence* is considered an oxymoron, the phrase *entertainment business* has some built-in paradoxes that need to be understood.

Emotion and logic join to produce a product. Too often people focus on one side or the other of this problematic equation without realizing that the two have to exist hand in hand.

I talked early in this book about your manuscript needing to appeal to both the intellect and the emotion of the reader. If it were just the former, we could reduce everything to a science, but because the latter comes into play, it becomes something of a guessing game.

How come Hollywood can't accurately predict the next blockbuster? How come publishers cannot accurately predict the next best seller?

I think that publishers throw a hundred books against the wall and hope one or two stick and sell well. In one year, up to thirty-five of forty new TV series from the past season can be canceled, so it's not just the publishing industry that plays this game.

The game is driven by numbers, which are driven by emotion. When all is said and done, success or failure is determined by number of copies sold. And it is an up or out business.

The first important number in the game is how many copies of your book the publisher is going to print. There is absolutely no way you are going to make *The New York Times* best-seller list with only twenty-five hundred hardcover copies printed, even if every single one sells.

There are two general ways a publisher determines the print run. For a new author, your advance will usually give you a very good idea of how many copies will be printed. (Many editors deny this, but this is my experience.)

For example, if you get a $10,000 advance, and you're being published in paperback original, here's the math: To earn out the advance, given that you get 8 percent list royalty of the cover price of $5.99 (which comes out to $0.4729 per book), 11,630 copies of your paperback have to sell. Given that the average current sell-through (the number sold versus the number printed) is about 50 percent on paperbacks, the publisher has to print 23,260 copies of the book. Guess what your print run will approximately be?

For a new author in hardcover, you usually don't make a percentage of the cover price, but a percentage of the wholesale (net) price. Let's say the royalty rate is 15 percent. So if your publisher is giving a 40 percent discount to the book chain, you make 15 percent of 60 percent of the cover price, which usually comes out to about $1.40 a book.

(Don't forget your agent is taking 15 percent of what you earn, but don't worry, only one out of ten books printed earns out its advance and sees royalties anyway.)

So, if you get a $10,000 advance for your hardcover, $10,000 divided by $1.40 equals 7,142 books have to sell to earn out. Assuming a 50 percent sell-through again, they'd have to print about 14,284 copies of your book.

Now that's for a new author. If you are an established author, the numbers are determined by previous sales. When the sales rep comes in with book number two, the first thing the book buyer does is check the computer and see what the sales figures were for book number one.

Let me give you a personal example of how to fail in this business and how numbers work: My first book was published as a hardcover. The advance was $7,500. The print run was 10,000 copies, which is pretty good for a new author. It sold about 7,500, which is 75 percent sell through. That percentage becomes critical, as you will see.

So, the sales reps for my publisher go out the following year to the book buyers and say, "Hey, we've got Bob Mayer's second book. How many do you want to order?"

The book buyer looks in his computer. He finds that he ordered ten per store of the first book, sold an average of seven. So how many does he order per store? You guessed it. Seven.

So the print run for my second hardcover was 7,500. It sold about 6,000 copies. An even better sell-through percentage but fewer copies. The third book had a print run of 6,000 and sold a higher percentage but fewer copies. By my sixth book with that publisher, I had failed.

Now how do you succeed?

Another personal example: My first paperback original with another publisher was under a new name, thus I was a "new" author (a good reason for pen names in this business).

My advance was $12,500. The print run was roughly 55,000 copies. It sold slightly more than 30,000 by the end of the first year. Not a bad sell-through but nothing to write home to mom about.

So the sales reps went out with the cover of the next book. What should have happened was the chains looked in their computer and ordered slightly less. But here's where something different came into play. The title on this new book, *Area 51*, was catchy. The cover design was intriguing. No one went overboard, but the orders came back strong. The initial print run for the second book had been scheduled for 55,000. With the strong orders, it got bumped in the weeks prior to printing. Until it finally settled at 80,000. They shipped 77,000 in the first week.

Within a couple of weeks they had to go back to print for 15,000 more. Then 20,000 more. Then 10,000, and then 20,000 more. In all, 135,000 were printed in the first year.

Guess what the print run for the next book in the series was? That's right, 135,000.

Numbers rule.

People always ask about royalties, but the fact is less than ten percent of books published earn royalties. First you have to earn back your advance. Enough books have to sell so that you make enough money to equal the advance you were given. Once you are past that, you begin to earn royalties.

Publishers are loath to pay out quicker than they have to, but it is a two-way street. While they tend to hold onto money for a long time after it is earned, they also pay advances long before they publish a book and earn any money. In the long run the two sort of balance out.

Typically publishers do semiannual accounting. The end of December accounting is credited at the earliest two months later, and in some cases three and a half months later. So technically, a publisher can hold onto money for six months, then an additional three and a half months which is getting pretty close to a year. Also, if you have subrights money coming, it can get bounced into another royalty period quite easily.

If I was a new writer and had a choice—which is highly unlikely—unless my advance was six figures, I would prefer to get published paperback first rather than hardcover. When was the last time you bought a hardcover book from a new author you never heard of?

Unless, of course, you get a large enough advance that it is obvious the publisher is really behind the book. Ultimately, your agent should be able to give you the best advice for your situation.

MARKETING AND SELF-PROMOTION

Your first book is finally published. You breathe a sigh of relief, lean back from your keyboard, and eagerly wait for the author's copies to arrive in the mail, while taking a long awaited break from work. Right? Only if you answer yes to one of the following two statements:

1. You received a large enough advance (that you won't have to pay back if your book does poorly) that you won't have to ever write again for money.

or:

2. You really don't care how many copies of your book sell, and you don't particularly want to make a living as a writer.

If you don't say yes to either of the above questions, then I regret to inform you that your work has only just begun.

The greatest mistake of most new authors is that they fail to properly market their first book. It took me four years to realize that the marketing side of being an author was just as important as the writing side, and it was only with my third novel that I finally got into the marketing side of the business. From going to book signings, to workshops, to doing publicity work, there are numerous ways you can market your work. Several books, including *The Writer's Market Companion* and *Writer's Market FAQs*, give good tips on how marketing.

PEN NAMES (OR WHO THE HELL ARE YOU ANYWAY?)

Why do I write under so many names? Currently, I am published under four names besides my own and have a manuscript on the market under a fifth name. The reasons are:

1. Normally, once you are under contract with a publisher, they "own" the next work under that name. The publisher has the right of first refusal on any new work, so you can only go elsewhere with it if they reject it. So to free yourself, you might have to use a different name.

2. You might be writing in a different genre. Readers and publishers are very picky. If you've been writing horror under your name for five years and suddenly write a romance, it would behoove you to use a different name to try to get it published. Very few authors have ever managed to switch genres under the same name.

   I once heard author Dan Simmons say he had been offered a unique contract—two books, any subject. That's very rare in the business. But Simmons has written horror and science fiction so well, the publisher felt whatever he wrote would work.

3. As I mentioned earlier, this is an up or out business. Using a new name gives you a new opportunity to succeed. When the book rep goes into the store with a book under a new pen name, you are more of a wild card than if they go in with a book under a name that has not sold well. Many authors have written under various pen names. Dean Koontz had several before consolidating as Dean Koontz.

   Are there guidelines for picking pen names? Not really. It's recommended you go early in the alphabet, since books are usually shelved according to authors' last names. I've started grouping my pen names in the Ds—Dalton, Doherty, Donegan. Makes it easier to look for the books in a store.

If you want to make writing your career, you have your foot on the first rung and it's a hard climb up. Figure out the strengths and weaknesses of your personality, and develop your marketing plan accordingly. If you are capable of walking into a bookstore, asking to see the manager, and then wooing him, go for it. If you're an Internet wizard and can put together a dazzling Web site and work mailing lists, then do that.

The paradox is that you must market your fiction, but you can't really market fiction. The first thing a marketing expert will tell you to do for a marketing plan is to figure out your target audience. For fiction this is rather difficult although not impossible.

TARGET YOUR MARKET

Unless you are fortunate and skilled enough to have a best seller, you are fighting for shelf space and time. You may not have noticed it before, but most books stay on the shelf a very short time. The person who cares the most about your book is not your editor or the marketing person (if there is one) at your publisher. It's you.

Different genres do have target audiences who have identified themselves as such. Some science fiction writers go to a lot of sci-fi conventions to market their work. If there is a specific group of people your book would appeal to, then try to find the media outlets that reach those people. When I was writing military thrillers I targeted publications such as *Army Times*. With my books about aliens I target outlets such as *UFO Magazine*.

BOOK SIGNINGS

Most new authors tend to overestimate how many books they will sell at a signing. Unless you have a best seller or a book that is of particular interest to the clientele of that store, you'll be lucky to sell a couple of copies of a $19.95 hardcover book. I've sat at signings for fourteen hours and sold zero copies of a book.

Because of that simple fact of life, you have to consider very carefully when and where to do signings. Not only is it very boring and somewhat discouraging to sit for six hours and only sell four books, it also takes valuable time away from your writing. When I wrote military techno-thrillers, I felt reasonably comfortable doing book signings at military post exchanges. Even then though, with a military population of almost forty thousand and twice that many dependents and retirees at a post, I considered twenty books sold in ten hours a good day.

You can do things to help the success of a signing. You may want to create a press release (described shortly). Or you might want to invest in a professionally done banner. (Don't expect the bookstore to strain itself by printing up posters and fliers, although many will. If you sell even fifty hardcover books, the bookstore's profit margin is not that great). You can also print up your own fliers or have postcards, fliers, and bookmarks printed professionally.

Consider talking with the bookstore manager when deciding whether or not to do a signing. I once tried setting up a book signing at the Pentagon bookstore. After talking to the employees though, and discovering the best signing they had was former Secretary of Defense Caspar Weinberger and he sold about a hundred books, I decided it would be a waste not only of my time, but of the store's. By making that decision I stayed in the good graces of the manager and can now bombard the store with press releases and fliers in the hopes that the manager will at least order more copies of my next book than he normally would have.

I've found there are several types of people you meet at a book signing. I've discovered that the longer someone talks to me, the less likely she is to buy a book. I usually meet a person who wants to get the "secret" from me of how to get published. Usually I answer questions for a while, and then tell him about this book. Since buying it would cost money, the person usually departs. There is also the person who wants to make a deal—she has a great idea and if I would only write it for her, she'd give me a certain percentage of the profits.

The biggest advantage of doing a signing is not so much to sell books, though, but to meet people. Although I sounded negative in the above paragraph, you do meet some interesting people at signings. Signings are a form of marketing in terms of networking.

PRESS RELEASES

To help market your book, you should create your own press releases. Talk to someone who works at a newspaper and enlist his aid. Or, go to the local university and talk to a faculty member in the journalism department.

A press release is a way to give a newspaper the information you want them to print in a format that they can use almost word for word (thus making it easier for them—and easy makes it more likely your information will get printed).

There are three basic press release boilerplates: (1) a release for a book signing; (2) a release for a new book coming out; and (3) a release for writing seminars you may teach.

Some basic rules:

1. Consider who you send the press release to. Why would they want to run it? A newspaper reports news—it doesn't give away free advertising space. For your local papers, emphasize the local angle. Press releases for book signings can have a local angle if the store is in the area. Keep in mind the editor who makes the decision on what to run. Give her a reason to put your information in the paper.
2. Put in a publicity photo of yourself. This can help to personalize your material.

3. Make the actual release very short, but include a full-page copy of your bio, fliers on books released (include reviews), and clips from your previous magazine publications (if you have any).

4. Address it by name to the appropriate editor. Many papers have special Sunday or even daily sections. Call the paper and ask who would be the best person to address the release to.

5. Get it there in *plenty of time* before you would like it to be printed. For newspapers, this will be at least a week, and for magazines, give yourself even more lead time (at least three to editions).

6. Follow up with a phone call about two or three days before the time it should go to print. Newspapers, even small ones, receive hundreds of releases. Your phone call may make the difference between it getting printed and not getting printed. Also it might help your release get noticed in the slush pile.

A MARKETING BINDER

A marketing binder is a very useful thing to have. Use it to keep most of your marketing resources close at hand. Mine contains such items as:

1. Fliers for all my books (separate ones for each and one covering all).

2. A mail-order form for my books. I also keep the form handy during book signings and use it as an ad in trade publications.

3. A one-page bio sheet. As noted above, it is very useful in conjunction with press releases. I also use it when interviewed—it answers most of the interviewer's questions up front and allows him to concentrate on the interview rather than writing down basic information. As a bonus, it also makes the interviewer's job easier, and everyone appreciates that.

4. A one-page flier for the writer's retreat I lead. This has come in useful at book fairs and signings—you'd be surprised who walks up to you.

5. A one-page flier for my "How to Get Published" seminar.

6. Clippings of articles I've had published.

7. Advertising fliers for my next book to be published. I give these out with every book I sell, even though the next book might be eight months away from being published.

8. One-page synopsis of every published book and every manuscript I have written.

9. Press clippings (articles written about me or my books).

10. Copies of my generic press releases.

11. A master listing of all points of contact.

12. Copies of reviews of all my published books.

13. 8½″ by 11″ business card inserts. These hold ten business cards on each side, so you can see them. You'd be surprised at the number of business cards you collect at workshops and signings. That's why it also pays to have your own to exchange.

As you can see this binder contains quite a bit, but it is very helpful to have all that material on hand whenever you go anywhere. Indeed, it's quite handy to simply have it all in one place even when you're working at your desk.

THE INTERNET

Consider marketing your work on the Internet. I've been doing this for several years and constantly am trying to improve. You have to be polite but aggressive when marketing yourself. No one else cares as much about your book as you do.

A PUBLICIST

What about hiring a publicist? I've asked quite a few people about this and the consensus for fiction is not to bother. Why? Because it's extremely hard to market fiction, which seems to contradict my telling you to market yourself. Let me clarify.

There really are no demographics for readers. I get e-mail from children and from grandparents. I have no clue who is really reading my books. Therefore a publicist is going to have a heck of a time doing one of the most important things she has to do before she can even start a publicity campaign: targeting your market. A legitimate publicity firm probably would not even take you on as a client if you write fiction.

But that doesn't mean you don't make the effort yourself. Doing this can be very frustrating because you never know what's working or not. And it's a long-term process. To really succeed in this business lightning has to strike you. Marketing is a form of raising a rod. It's not a guarantee you'll get hit, but it makes the odds better.

Now, to further muddy an already murky picture, let me talk about something I've learned late in my writing career:

Answer the following question: Why did you buy the last novel you bought?

A. I had read the author before and liked him.

B. Someone recommended the book to me.

C. Never read this author before but I noticed the title/jacket, and read the cover blurb and the first couple of pages, and thought I might like it.

D. I read a review of the book.

E. The author was doing a book signing locally, and I bought a copy.

F. The author received a six-figure advance.

G. The publisher placed an ad in *Publishers Weekly*.

The answers are listed in this order for a specific reason. Surveys have shown that this is the order in which the majority of readers buy books. Most buy books by author name. Then by recommendation.

This survey was put out at a conference by Donald Maass, a literary agent and author of *Writing the Breakout Novel*, to make a point—authors who get wrapped up in the size of their advance and the publicity effort made by their publisher often miss the boat. I spent a lot of time spinning my wheels trying to get publishers to allocate money and time to publicity for my books. Much of that was wasted time. That's not to say you shouldn't try to get as much publicity and support as possible, but it is to say that ultimately the book has to sell. The number one thing a publisher does for a book after it's printed is to get it out to the stores. Once you are on the rack or bookshelf, readers determine your career.

I used to get very frustrated talking to my editor or publicist because he would say, "We put the majority of our publishing time and money behind our best-selling books." And my angry reply would be: "How am I going to become one of your best-selling authors if you don't give me any publicity?" That has a certain ring of logic to it, but I've since changed my tune. Publicity is not going to make you a best seller by itself. And many times, much more than most people imagine, most best-selling authors work their way into that status by selling a little more of each book, year after year.

There is a thin line that a writer has to follow in terms of making a book a success. The most important factor is to write an interesting, good book. You must do your own publicity work, but you must also be very cognizant of how much time and resources you are going to put into it against the returns you will get. You also have to be careful of crossing the line from being aggressive to being obnoxious. Always try to be polite in your dealings with people.

DEALING WITH YOUR CONTACTS

Like any business, be professional with everyone you deal with. That includes agents, publishers, booksellers, bookstore owners, and writers' groups. Networking is very important for authors, and you will be surprised at what benefits you will reap if you deal courteously and professionally with all you meet.

Just today I received a letter from a man I met at one of my book signings—turns out he had his own book in print and also wrote a column in a local paper, and he kindly reviewed my book. Every little bit helps.

Keep good records of all your correspondence. Make a copy of everything, and maintain accurate files so you can find documents when needed. Also keep good track of your due dates and try to beat them when at all possible.

I often get e-mail or letters from people who want help. Some want me to ghostwrite a great idea they have. There are very few writers who would be willing to do this. Most have their own work to do and the odds of such a book getting published are usually slim. Remember, whether you are trying to get published or you are published, time is money. There is a tendency for people who are self-employed to forget this, but authors have to value their time.

Be careful of approaching people cold. Also, if you do make a contact, don't be too aggressive. I told a fellow who contacted me one time to send me a one-page synopsis, and he shipped me the entire manuscript. That was a fast turnoff. Additionally, when sending requested material, don't make anyone go out of his way to get it—using a delivery system that requires the receiver to go to the post office to sign for it is a sure way to irritate a potential contact.

Always remember to thank any contacts you make and remain positive.

BASIC MARKETING RULES

Title is critical. It is the number one marketing tool you have a large degree of control over. Come up with a title that makes the reader want to pull a book off the shelf. While you may not have ultimate control over this, present your publisher with something strong. Mary Higgins Clark says a title should invite you into the book. Many authors come up with a title that only makes sense if you read the book. That's backward logic. No one is going to read a book from an unknown author unless the title draws her in. Spending a considerable amount of time finding the right title for your novel.

Here are some other basic rules about marketing a novel:

1. Write the best book you can. Word of mouth makes or breaks authors.
2. Go primarily for media outlets, such as radio, newspaper, and magazines.
3. Put together a Web site with an easy address that people can remember.
4. Have available a flyer promoting your book and you.
5. Teach classes, go to conferences, and network.
6. Recognize that if you don't do it for yourself, no one else will.

GENRE

Part of identifying your book's market is to understand genre. The more you write about ordinary life, the more extraordinary your writing must be. People live everyday life. To take them into it and engross them, you must be a superb writer. If you write about extraordinary events, then the quality of writing does not necessarily need to rise to this same high standard. I'm not saying you can be bad, but I am saying you can count on the core of the story to engross the reader.

Decide where your book fits (if it does fit). No one likes hearing it, but there are certain guidelines to follow when writing in specific fields. If you are writing an action/suspense novel, then your primary emphasis is on action. That doesn't mean your book shouldn't have good characterization, but you should not emphasize the characters at the expense of slowing down the action. Remember the perspective of the reader: When he buys your book, or picks it up to read, why does he do that? What is he looking for?

You should be intimately familiar with the bookstore section in which you write. Know who the authors are. Know who the publishers are. Consider joining an appropriate writer's group, e.g., Sisters in Crime for those interested in female mystery writers. Optimally, you should go to a writers conference where a writer in your field will be and try to get information firsthand. Go to the library and review copies of *Publishers Weekly*. Read the book reviews and articles to see what is being published.

I am not saying your writing has to fit into a genre. I am simply saying that most books do. The Romance Writers of America (RWA) publishes statistics on genre book sales that you should be aware of:

» Romance: 55.9 percent of all fiction sold in North America. Mystery/Detective/Suspense: 28.1 percent of all fiction sold in North America.
» Science Fiction/Fantasy: 7.2 percent of all fiction sold in North America.

That only leaves 8.8 percent for everything else.

If you look at the recent history of publishing, there are certain names that stick out: King, Clancy, Crichton, Grisham, etc. What these writers have in common is that they each basically launched a new genre. That's not to say that there weren't horror books before Stephen King, but it is to say that somehow King did something a little different—a stronger focus on characters—and broke open the field.

Sometimes when I talk to other writers, I realize that pretty much everything has been done before. The secret is to do it better and/or do it slightly different with a new twist.

That said, though, you really cannot try to anticipate the marketplace. For most authors, the lag time between concept generation and bookstore placement averages around three years. So while lawyer books might be hot this year, don't count on them being hot by the time you get your book done and marketed. *Write what you can write and what you want to write.* Study your genre to see what has been done and how it can help you do what you want to.

There are times when you don't want to fit in a genre. One of my publishers doesn't want to list my Area 51 series of books as science fiction because he feels the books can reach a broader audience if they're labeled mainstream. Mainstream is where everything goes that doesn't definitively fit into one of the categories of genre—science fiction, fantasy, mystery, and romance.

Your story does not have to be enjoyed by everyone. If you are writing a romance, and you hand it to someone who has never read—nor likes—romance novels, to read and critique, don't expect very good feedback. If one person in ten out of your writers group says, "Hey, I really liked that," then think about it—10 percent of the selected population liked your story. If 10 percent, or even 1 percent, of the people who enter a bookstore wants to buy it, then you have a best seller.

Earlier I mentioned that it seems like most aspiring writers (and writing programs) disdain genre and try to write books about life. I always suggest that a new novelist write a genre novel or two before moving on to the Great American Novel—it is like an architecture professor giving his student a set of blueprints and saying, "Here's a rough set of guidelines of buildings like the one you want to build, and all these guidelines worked. Now, use these as a reference and design your own."

Putting a novel together is so difficult that any way you can help yourself in the beginning is useful and use a familiar subject and format will help you. If you read five romance novels a week, then you have "studied" romance writing quite a bit. You know the format. You know the flow of the book. You even know quite a bit about the business end—the authors, publishers, and the market.

To better understand genre, consider joining a specialized writing group. There are writers' groups for most genres, e.g., Sisters In Crime for those interested in female mystery writers (for more information, see Appendix D). There are science-fiction groups, mystery groups, and fantasy groups. There are also conventions and workshops designed specifically for those areas, such as the Boucheron conference for mystery writers. The Romance Writers of America is an extremely professional and well-run group as well, and they have an annual nationwide convention along with smaller, local ones.

WRITING SCAMS

Because writing involves a lot of emotion, naturally there are those who prey on others in the business.

As an aspiring author, you should beware of shady agents. Here are some of the warning signs:

» Has a P.O. box for an address. Such addresses are easy to set up and also can disappear overnight.
» Solicits by direct mail. Very few agents send out mailings hoping to find a client.

» Won't give you a client list or at least a referral to a client.

» Owns its own "publishing" house.

» Charges an up-front fee. Some legitimate agencies that *are not* fee charging will charge you for some costs such as copying manuscripts and postage. But this cost should not include a reading fee. Some fee-charging agencies are getting slicker and try to hide their reading fee in such normally legitimate expenses as copying and postage. Use your common sense to examine costs.

» Commission rate exceeds 15 percent for North American rights.

» Guarantees to get you published. No legitimate agent can do that. I've seen this in print from some agencies, and the best I can figure is that they have a deal with a self-publishing house. Thus, if you're willing to pay, well, the guarantee wasn't a lie.

» Can't refer to any sales with legitimate publishers.

» If it sounds too good to be true, it is. There are sites on the Net where you can find listings of agencies that are suspicious or have done shady practices. You have to do your homework.

» Refers you to a book doctor. The latter is a scam that has been going on for a while. Recently, a company was caught in an interesting scam involving this. It set up bogus agencies and publishing companies, which referred every single query back to itself for book doctoring. Regardless of the quality of the query, these agencies and "publishers" send you a form letter saying that your manuscript was close to being publishable but still needed some work. They then recommended you work with their own company.

Which leads us to the issue of book doctors. Many new writers find themselves in a catch-22. Since there is no real apprenticeship system, many writers are desperate for some feedback, an idea of how good their work really is.

There are some legitimate people out there who edit manuscripts for a fee. My recommendation: Most legitimate editors should be able to tell what is wrong with your manuscript by looking at a cover letter, synopsis, and fifteen or so pages—i.e., by looking at a submission. They shouldn't need to see all four hundred pages. Neither does a book doctor. So if you have to pay, only have them review a part of the manuscript, which might save you money.

Another thing to remember, though, is getting honest feedback can be painful. If you just want a pat on the back, you're looking in the wrong direction.

WRITING GROUPS, CONFERENCES, AND PROGRAMS

Writing tends to be a solitary profession and, as mentioned earlier, one without a real apprenticeship program where you can make a living while learning the craft. Writing groups, conferences, and writing programs try to address some of these problems. There are pros and cons to each, but the final verdict on whether one is right for you depends on what you want.

WRITING GROUPS

Writing groups are usually local; several people who enjoy writing band together and start meeting once a month or so. They read to each other and give feedback. Occasionally they bring in different speakers for presentations.

Groups usually have different focuses—short stories, poetry, and novels are the three basic areas. Some groups try to do all areas; with this type you may have to sit through writing you might not particularly be interested in, but here lies a hidden advantage: As a novelist, if you have an open mind, you will learn something by listening to poets or short story writers. You can learn about perspective, the craft of those other mediums, and about people—not just through the written word but also by observing those who do the writing. Poets, short story writers, novelists, songwriters—they all speak some common language, but there are different angles for each area that can add to your repertoire.

I have found, though, that the people who get the least out of the typical writers' group are the novelists. It is very difficult to read a chapter from a novel and get a good critique, especially if you aren't reading the opening chapter. You have to get people up to speed on the story, then have to weather all the "Why didn't you . . ." questions. About one out of ten of those questions are worthwhile. While there are definite advantages to attending writing groups, be aware of the difficulty of reading from a novel in progress at such a group.

A novelist needs assistance with her work. I'm a believer in talking with friends who are well read and other writers. As far as a formal group goes, it depends on if being in the group energizes you or drains you. Make sure you aren't in a group where it's a case of the blind leading the blind. Also, are you just talking about your book, or are you writing it?

For a writing group (and writing class) to survive there should be no critiquing of the subject matter an author chooses to write about. Nothing can tear a group apart quicker than people wading into the subject matter—I saw one group run off several writers whose subject matter was religious. The discussion didn't center on the way the person had written the material, but rather became a theological discussion about the material itself. In the same manner, open-mindedness must exist about such things as sex, "profane" language, and political views.

Some writers benefit greatly from critique groups; others not at all. You have to find what works best for you. As I said earlier, the best editor for a book is usually the writer, if the writer is willing to be honest with herself.

CONFERENCES

You can find out about local and national conferences in *Writer's Market* or online at http://shawguides.com.

Conferences are the key to networking, and publishing is like any other business—who you know is sometimes almost as important as what you do. There is a difference in the way a cold query is treated versus a query an editor or agent can put a face to. You also get to put a face to editors and agents.

When you attend a conference, consider the motives of the people who attend. Why are these writers here? Two main reasons are to make some money and to do the same thing you are, network.

Why are these editors here? To look for new writers? Mostly, but I know an editor who has been doing several conferences a year for more than a dozen years and has only picked up two properties. To get out of the office? To network with the *other* editors and agents at the conference? To get a free plane ticket and lodging? There are a number of possible reasons. The same is true of agents. At conferences, I have also seen fee-charging agents who are there to drum up business. Again, this is not necessarily bad depending on what *you* want.

Best-selling science fiction author Harlan Ellison is well known for eviscerating writers when he holds writing classes. His point is that writing is his profession and those who want to enter it have to be very, very good. He has little patience for those who approach it without the highest standards. When working with other writers, I try to be as honest as possible without being rude. Giving false praise wastes everyone's time, but occasionally there are people who do not like hearing anything negative about their project. There are some people who get perturbed that the instructors, editors, and agents do not do more to "encourage" the writers. As one editor responded, that that wasn't his job—that was the writer's job.

If you do go to a conference, be prepared. Many have sign-ups where you get to talk to an editor or agent for fifteen minutes. Rehearse what you are going to say. Have your cover letter and one-page synopsis in hand. Pitch your idea and story succinctly and in an interesting manner. Don't expect to hand the manuscript to them—remember, most are flying home and don't have the space or desire to haul it with them on the plane.

When you get feedback, consider it carefully. Don't argue. It won't change their mind about your book, but it will make them think you would be hard to work with.

Use the free time constructively. At a conference I once attended, I sat for two hours in the bar one evening talking with a fellow who had been Bob Hope's top writer for years, picking up information and advice about the business. What amazed me was that all the nights I was there, not a single attendee wandered in and sat down and chatted with the authors, editors, and agents who were stuck in the motel. When the conference director asks for people who want to pick up agents and editors at the airport, be willing to volunteer. Take them out to dinner. You might be surprised at what you will reap. I've learned more over a one-hour dinner with editors than sitting for four hours in their lecture during the day.

Treat the people who run the conference with respect and courtesy. They are volunteers who have given tremendously of their time and effort to make sure the conference works. It's not their fault the hotel service is bad or that an author or editor missed a meeting.

When you have to make a choice between workshops, focus more on those given by writers rather than editors and agents. Go to workshops given by people who are where you want to be. When asking questions in a workshop or panel, try to make them generic rather than "I've just written a book about x, y, and z, and I want to know. . . ."

Sell yourself if you have something to sell. For example, I once worked with a writer whose husband had been a Formula One race car driver; she was writing a thriller based in that world. She had something to talk about that most people knew little about.

Do people actually get discovered at conferences? Yes. I just received an e-mail from a successful writer who told me how he got his first book contract set up at a conference. A few months ago, a man who was in my group at the Maui Writers Retreat e-mailed me to tell me of his two-book deal.

I'm getting toward the close of this book, and this issue of conferences brings up something that dovetails into what I've written on all these pages. I once listened to an agent talk about mid-career writers and the mistakes they make. The next morning I saw him at breakfast, and I told him what he had said the previous day had really struck home. The interesting thing, I continued, was that if I had heard what he'd said a year earlier, I would have understood it intellectually, but I wouldn't have accepted it emotionally.

This level of comprehension is a critical aspect of being a writer. You might have nodded at much of what I've written in this book and said to yourself, "Well, that's common sense." But do you really believe it? There is a gap between understanding and acceptance. That gap can cause not just writers, but anyone, great trouble in their life. My second agent never confronted me about anything. Also, he sometimes wouldn't give me advice when I asked for it. I've realized it wasn't because he was bored or didn't have time, but rather, like a good psychologist, he pointed me in the right direction, but he knew that whether I decided to go there or not was totally up to me. In fact, if he did give me advice I wasn't ready to hear, I could have ended up reacting and going totally in the wrong direction.

It's a good idea for you to reread this book after a time period to see if some of what is in it strikes you differently as you write more and more.

WRITING PROGRAMS

If you're looking for something close to a writing apprenticeship, consider an MFA program (master of fine arts in creative writing). These programs usually focus on the creative side of writing. There are some excellent ones, such as the University of Iowa's. While most view an MFA as a rather large investment of time and money, remember that writing is a serious business and no matter which path you take, you will have to invest considerable time, effort, and money. Another advantage of MFA programs is that once you get your degree, you have an inside track for teaching jobs at other MFA programs.

There are other schools such as the Writer's Online Workshop from Writer's Digest. I've taught in the program, and it's a worthwhile course if you're willing to learn. Unfortunately many people who sign up for it seem to want a stamp of approval for their work and then move on immediately to getting and agent and being published. With the school, the instructors are published authors so they understand the business side of writing. You get as much out of it as you put in.

HOLLYWOOD, MOVIE RIGHTS, AND SCREENPLAYS

If you've never been to Los Angeles, Hollywood in particular, it's hard to describe. There is a rather strange atmosphere in the air. I love the smell of movie rights in the morning. The city smells of money.

Right. And if pigs had wings, they'd fly. Certainly there are big bucks to be made in Hollywood, but books being optioned for millions are few and far between. The common option on a book is a couple of thousand and nothing ever happens. But that's not to say you can't dream.

What is an option? An option gives whoever buys it ownership for the theatrical rights to a work for a given period of time. That person usually then goes around and tries to sell the work to a studio.

Think of some rather famous books and how long it took for them to get made. *Interview With the Vampire* made the rounds for many years, and several different people, including Julia Phillips—the first woman to win an Oscar as producer (*Close Encounters of the Third Kind*)—held the option for a period of time. Read her book *You'll Never Eat Lunch in This Town Again* to get an idea of how Hollywood works.

The longer I've worked with various Hollywood types, the more amazed I am that any movie ever gets made. It's a brutal business, and the amount of commitment needed by any involved party in order to see a project through to completion is phenomenal.

I've noticed a recent trend where people ask me for free options, contingent on the fact that they will take the work and try to market it. I've done this a couple of times, but I will never do it again as people don't respect something that they get for free.

However, you do have to be amenable. The production company that owned the option on one of my books called and said they wanted to renew the option, but they didn't want to pay all of the money owed up front. I agreed because I felt they were doing a good job trying to get the film made.

An agent is usually the one who will handle negotiating an option for you. Also, most literary agents have a connection with film agents so they can market your book for option.

→TOOL:10

YOUR FUTURE

E-BOOKS, PRINT ON DEMAND, AND THE FUTURE

Where is publishing heading? Its future definitely affects everyone from writers through readers.

The biggest problem in publishing right now is inventory and shipping. Every time you walk into a store and buy a paperback, you're actually paying for two or three. As I discussed in chapter nine, the average sell-through for paperbacks hovers somewhere around 50 percent or lower. What happens to the ones that don't sell? They get the cover torn off for credit, and then they're recycled. This can result in large losses for the publisher.

Bookstores are a retail business that can return the product, so basically they are consignment stores. Therefore the priority is to move products through shelf space, not necessarily to sell a specific book. The time that stores leave books on their shelves before they decide to replace it with something else is growing shorter and shorter.

Two trends have emerged that might alleviate this problem. One is electronic publishing. The book is downloaded, so you can read it on your computer or on specially designed handheld displays that open one page at a time on the screen. While this can solve publishers' problems with unsold books, it raises some problems for authors. If a book is in electronic form and can be printed at the push of a button, publishers can rightly claim the book is never out of print. (I talk more about that a little further on.)

The second trend is print on demand (POD). With POD, bookstores are able to quickly print and bind books as needed. This could alleviate the problem of large inventory and returns.

Another interesting trend is the resurgence of small presses. As the larger publishing houses become more concerned with the bottom line and best sellers, smaller houses are able to take over the midlist. With online bookstores and the possibility of POD, these smaller publishers make be able to take a larger piece of the market.

Publishing is on the edge of a lot of big changes, and anyone who wants to be an author should stay on top of these changes because they will affect everyone involved in the business.

ELECTRONIC BOOKS

We will always have the printed book. It is the traditional medium and the one most people prefer by far. E-books are more than just a traditional book. They are living books. With an e-book, you can cross-reference, underline, make notes, have a dictionary handy, highlight, and even have video and pictures to supplement the story. You also can increase the size of fonts so that any book can be a large print book.

Textbooks would seem to make for ideal e-books. Instead of lugging around fifty pounds of books, a student could load all his texts into one handheld device.

Of course a breakthrough in the popularity might come when all the various pieces of hardware, the e-book, laptop, Palm Pilot, and cell phone, are scrunched into one device. Think about the possibilities. With one machine you could:

» Book your flight and room.
» Read an e-book on the flight.
» Bring up a map to make sure you know where you are (and probably use a ground-positioning receiver to pinpoint your location).
» Look up references for various sites you visit.
» Type in notes about what you see (so you can tax-deduct the trip).

At the present, though, the future of e-books seems shaky. Random House has discontinued its e-book imprint. The Frankfurt eBook Award also has been discontinued. Time-Warner's e-book imprint iPublish was closed in 2001. I've already mentioned that numbers rule and at present, the numbers have not appeared for e-books.

The future of the e-book might be linked with the next generation that is more familiar with reading off screens than our generation. (Notice, however, the Harry Potter books are still bound traditionally.)

SELF-PUBLISHING

They're called "vanity presses" for a reason. Pay if you simply want to feel good about having a bound book. A tiny fraction of self-published books turn a profit. If it was such a good book, the odds are a regular publisher would have taken it on. Like literary agencies that charge a fee, vanity presses make their money off of you, not the book.

Even though they use the same technology, there is a difference between a vanity press and POD. POD produces a trade paperback book from an electronic file at a reasonable cost. This allows a single copy of a book to be printed. Standard printers for hardcover or mass-market paperback books require large print runs to be economically feasible. As more POD machines are made and the technology improves, there will come a day when almost every bookstore will have one in the back, which will reduce the problem of shipping and returns.

A vanity press uses POD technology, but charges you to produce the book. The real trap in self-publishing is marketing your book. Most bookstore chains won't even give you the time of day. For 99.9 percent of you reading this, forget about self-publishing. Currently, Barnes & Noble has a blanket policy of not stocking any self-published books.

I recently sat next to a self-published author at a book fair. He was a sports columnist for a local paper who took a bunch of his articles and made a book out of them. The first thing he did right was not expend a whole lot of energy in writing a book, since the work was already done. He had five hundred copies printed up and sold them at local book fairs across Kentucky and was doing all right. He also visited local bookstores and had his book placed in there on commission. He's an example of self-publishing working well. If you are sure you can market and sell your book, then self-publishing might be for you—this mostly applies to specific nonfiction markets.

Self-publishing is one of the fastest growing businesses. But that doesn't mean the books that are self-published are making money. It means the people who get paid to publish those books have more clients. Big difference.

Another time self-publishing is good is when you simply want to have a book in hand that you can give to people, perhaps your family.

If you've written your memoirs, it might be a good idea to get it published and bound so you can give it to your children and great-grandchildren.

Currently, a number of POD publishers straddle the line between vanity press and regular press. They offer writers an easy way out. Instead of sucking it up and wading through the hundreds of rejections and continuing to improve, many new writers settle for being published by one of these presses. They don't crawl over the razor's edge of rejection and improvement that is needed to become a true artist. When I started out writing, this option wasn't available. A writer nowadays can be seduced too easily by the path more often traveled but that leads essentially nowhere.

Know your objective, go for it, and don't allow the easier way to distract or derail you.

GETTING STARTED

This section may appear to be in the wrong place. Most how-to-write books place it in the beginning—after all, if you don't start, how can you ever do anything?

I place this near the end because I don't think it does you much good to start unless you understand what you're starting. Some of you may already have completed manuscripts; others may not have put word one down on paper. The first half of this book gives you the tools to start and complete a novel. The willpower is up to you. The second half gives you the information you need to submit your completed work and get it published.

What about something in between, though? What about getting some publishing credit before finishing the epic novel (something that may even help the sale of the novel)?

Most creative writing classes focus on the short story as the basic building block. I believe a good short story is much harder to write than a good chapter in a novel. In a short story, you have to complete the story, whereas the chapter is just a continuation of a longer story. Also, a short story is usually better written style-wise than a chapter in a novel simply because there is more focus on the language.

However, it is extremely difficult in the present market to sell short fiction. Top-notch freelancers with glittering résumés already supply the top of the line magazines, and the bottom of the line doesn't pay you for your work. And, although the short story market is starting to pick up a little bit, there doesn't appear to be much middle of the line in the short fiction magazine world.

If you want to write a novel, then write a novel. Don't spin your wheels writing short stories unless you feel you need the practice in writing. Don't get me wrong—it is certainly excellent practice, but don't look at it as a way to make money unless you are very good. Short story writing skills don't necessarily translate into successful novel writing.

If you do want to get published in a magazine, try to write and sell nonfiction articles. When I suggest this to my students, the first question I always get back is, "I'm just a student/housewife/candle-stick-maker. What could I write about?" My usual response: "Well, write about school/home/the candlestick business." Pull out your atlas and look around at a hundred-mile radius of your home. Is there any place interesting that you might be able to write about?

So far, my articles have been about—you guessed it—writing. But to start with, I narrowed my area down. I combined my two careers, writing and the military, and sold an article about writing for military members to *Life in the Times*, a supplement to the *Army Times*, the *AirForce Times*, and the *Navy Times*. Know your marketplace. No matter how great a writer you are, if you don't have an idea how to operate as a businessperson, you aren't going to get very far.

The economics of becoming a writer is very difficult. Even if you get a manuscript accepted for publication, the odds are very strong that you still won't be making a living from writing. Many people have the talent—not many have the courage and fortitude to go where that talent can take them without any guarantees of success.

Not only does it take time, but there are no job openings with salaries in the classified section of the newspaper. (Of course there are some jobs that are writing related, but I've never seen an advertisement for "unpublished author" yet.)

What would I do if I were an unpublished author with a complete manuscript right now?

Start writing a second manuscript. As I discussed earlier, too many writers get caught up on marketing their one and only manuscript that they put all their eggs in one basket. You've learned so much from writing the first one the best thing is to put all that to work in writing a second one. Also, remember, you might want to be well into your second manuscript in case you're offered a two-book contract.

To market that first manuscript (while I'm putting most of my energy into writing the second one), I would:

1. Write a good cover letter.
2. Write a good one-page synopsis.
3. Research agents and editors, and make a list of agents (non-fee charging) and publishers (ranging from the big ones in New York, to the one down the street working out of a garage). Mail to five agents and five publishers on week one. Then another five agents and five publishers in a week or two. Keep that up until you run out of agents and publishers. This way you spread out the rejections (just joking). This way you keep your hopes up.

I would also try to attend a writing conference where I might meet some editors, agents, and authors.

And then, I would never quit.

BREAKING OUT

In an interview in *USA Weekend* (January 7-9, 1994), Michael Crichton said, "I read somewhere that there are only about two hundred Americans who can make a living from writing full time. I thought: I can't be one of two hundred people in America. That's too hard." He's talking about his early years, when he was faced with the decision between becoming a writer or going to medical school. His choice was medical school.

The current state of published writing in America right now is a strange mixture. There are three main types of writers:

1. **Best-selling authors.** These are the writers who command megabucks, and their books are guaranteed to be best sellers even before they write them.
2. **Literary writers.** These are the authors who usually sell few copies, are well received critically, and make their living teaching in the university system or off of grants. Most literary writers publicly disdain the first group and ignore the third.
3. **The pack.** These are the authors who write mainstream/genre fiction and who scrape their way from $5,000 advance to $5,000 advance; this money is received only after the manuscript has been written and rejected on average by fifteen to forty publishers. Most members of the pack strive to become part of the first group and are too busy writing to make much sense of the second group.

I've talked to other midlist writers, and many of them harbor some resentment toward the first group. I think that feeling is misplaced. One friend of mine broke down Stephen King's latest multimillion dollar advance into how much fifty authors could each get, but the fact of the matter is those fifty authors probably wouldn't sell as many books combined as Stephen King.

A writer like Stephen King, John Grisham, or Sue Grafton supports a lot of beginning and midlist writers by helping publishing houses make enough profit to publish another writer's first novel. The big names pick up financial slack for the publisher.

Literary writers and members of the pack follow different writing routes, although the "streams can be crossed," to misquote *Ghostbusters*, without a nuclear meltdown. The literary/academic world usually requires one of two things: a master's degree in writing or winning a prestigious award or grant. It is a somewhat closed circle, and to enter, you usually need to start at the bottom, i.e., attend a master's program. A master's program is a doorway into the academic writing life and the most readily accessible one (given you have the time and money to participate).

The pack is also a very difficult group to enter, and an even more difficult one to remain in. An advantage of entering the academic world is that you can gain a certain degree of security as you climb each rung. Ninety-five percent of writers in the pack perish *after* publishing their first novel. Some hang on by sheer quantity of work—e.g. if the average novel commands a $5,000- to $10,000-advance, they write several "average" novels per year under many names to sustain themselves. That sort of living can be quite tasking, though. Most writers in the pack have a job in addition to writing.

Others get struck by lightning and break through to the first group. Congratulations. This is often as much due to luck as skill, but don't begrudge any of those who make it because they did the legwork in order to get "lucky." You don't get lucky in the writing world doing nothing. If you worked hard enough, had a little bit of luck, and finally sold your first novel, there are many traps you have to be aware of. The work has just begun.

The first trap is thinking that you've got it made. Unless your advance was significant, you have to remember one of the rules of the publishing world: Advance roughly equals copies printed, which roughly equals one-half of copies sold, which roughly, hopefully, earns the advance back. If you have a $10,000 advance and think to yourself, "This is going to hit *The New York Times* best-seller list and sell 250,000 copies hardcover," you've got a rude awakening coming. A $10,000 advance for a hardcover book might entail a first run of three to four thousand books. You can't sell more books than they print. Keep writing.

Another trap involves the track the book selling and publishing world pushes writers into. If your first three books all do moderately well and each sells, say, 40,000 out of a 75,000 paperback run, guess what? They probably aren't going to print 300,000 copies of your fourth book. In my experience, I've found that publishers tend to cut down on the print run the longer I am with them as they see they don't have a best-seller but a rather solid lower level book. Publishers tend to be willing to take more of a risk on a new unknown author than an established mediocre one. Every once in a while though, publishers reach out and give the golden nod to one of their midlist writers to move up, but that's usually because the writer delivered a manuscript that made the leap in terms of quality compared to previous work.

Bookstores and book suppliers, such as Ingram, own computers— those same contraptions that many of us writers use to produce our work. However, they use their computers differently. They track books, authors, and sales, and punch all that into the machines. Then, using a toad's eye, a rabbit's foot, blood of a bat, and a few freelance witches, they (ever notice how there is always a *they,* no matter what line of work you are in?) decide how many of each book they are going to order, which in turn causes the necromancers at your publisher to decide how many they are going to print. Once you establish a track record, breaking out of it is difficult.

Unless you have a best-selling book, the road usually leads down, which can be discouraging. But it is possible to beat the odds. It takes luck, which comes from the application of hard work. It also takes willingness to change and become a better writer and a better business-person in the writing world.

You have to be willing do whatever it takes, even though some-times it can get quite tedious and irritating. Nobody said it was going to be easy, and it isn't. As a corner man might say to a boxer who is getting beaten and bloodied in the ring, you gotta' want it, kid.

There is a classic story of a young fellow who was interested in playing violin. He studied for many years and finally got his big break to play before the "master." He played his heart out, and when he was done, he asked the master what he thought. The master replied, "Not enough fire," then left.

The young man was crushed. He put his violin away and pursued another career. Years later, he met the master at a social gathering. He cornered him and reminded him of the event many years ago, saying that the master's somewhat less than inspiring comment had caused him to give up the violin and change his life. The master was surprised. "I tell everyone that," he informed the young man, "regardless of how well they play. If my comment so easily dissuaded you, then you didn't want it badly enough and didn't believe in yourself enough."

You will have plenty of opportunities to quit writing and not many to continue. The choice is always yours.

IN CLOSING

Quite a bit of what you just read won't make much sense to you if you are just beginning to write manuscripts. But reread it every once in a while, and you will find that the more you write, the more sense it makes. I read numerous writing books when I first began and got quite frustrated because a lot of it seemed very simple, or I didn't agree with some of the things that were said. But I didn't truly understand until I tried writing. Then all the advice began clicking into place.

Remember that writing is work. You must put the time and effort into it to succeed.

So, although I said there is no right or wrong, I will leave you with one simple rule:

Write.

Then . . . write some more.

Then . . . yep, write even more.

APPENDIX A: SAMPLE CHAPTER OUTLINE

CHAPTER 1

Nashville/9 Nov/11 PM/0400 Zulu

» Kelly Reynolds gets a tape and letter in mail from a male reporter friend as she comes home late at night.

» She listens to the tape—intercepted radio conversation between AF jet pilot participating in Red Flag (U.S. vs. "Soviet" simulation flight out of Nellis AFB) getting caught by tower (Dreamland—Nellis AFB call sign) for violating restricted air space over Area 51. Pilot reports being forced down by strange object, then goes off air suddenly. Male friend says he is going to investigate—will be there on such and such night—the same night she is listening to the tape.

Nellis Air Force Base Range/9 Nov/10 PM/0600 Zulu

» Shift to male reporter infiltrating site 51 in Nevada.

The Cube, Area 51/9 Nov/10:30 PM/0630 Zulu

» Shift to underground government building (the Cube = C3 = CCC, Command and Control Central) where they pick up the man infiltrating on IR scope from nearby mountain and track him coming in. Introduce General Gullick; refer to pending Nightscape mission; start recall.

Purpose: introduces Kelly, Area 51 site mystery.

APPENDIX B: SAMPLE COVER LETTER

Presidio Press   29 April 2000
31 Pamaron Way
Novato, CA 94949

Dear Ms. _____

What if a secret organization of West Point graduates has been covertly manipulating our government's policies for the past fifty years and now appears to be planning a coup against the President?

THE LINE is the story of Boomer Watson, an officer in the Army's elite Delta Force, and Major Benita Trace, assigned to a headquarters in Hawaii where the President will be arriving in one week to give a speech at the fifty-sixth anniversary of the attack on Pearl Harbor. Each stumbles across clues pointing to both the existence of The Line and the apparent coup. When they get together, they realize it is up to them to stop the impending assassination.

I have eight novels accepted for publication, three of which have been published. As specific background for this novel, I graduated from West Point in 1981 and served in the Green Berets as an A-Team Leader and Battalion Operations Officer for ten years.

This is a 100,000-word thriller. I appreciate you taking the time to review this submission and look forward to hearing from you.

Sincerely,

APPENDIX C: SAMPLE SYNOPSIS

THE LINE

What if a secret military organization has been covertly manipulating our government's policies for the past fifty years and now appears to be planning a coup?

BOOMER WATSON is a member of the Delta Force on a classified mission into the Ukraine when everything goes wrong. Returning from the apparently botched mission, Boomer is relieved of his command and sent to Hawaii to get him out of the way. In Hawaii, he links up with a former lover and fellow West Pointer, MAJOR BENITA TRACE, who is working on a novel about an organization she calls THE LINE, referring to the long gray line of West Point graduates.

Boomer becomes aware that strange events are occurring. A commander is relieved and a right wing officer takes his place; a covert special operations mission is being planned to coincide with the President's visit to Pearl Harbor on December 7th, where the President will make a speech on his Military Reform Act, which is violently opposed by the military; the Colonel from the office of the Joint Chiefs of Staff who ordered the ill-fated mission in the Ukraine suddenly shows up in Hawaii; a Sergeant Major tells Boomer the story of Boomer's father's death in Vietnam, a story that coincides with Trace's suspicions about The Line.

When Trace's house is broken into and the manuscript is stolen, Boomer goes to the north shore of Oahu and observes a classified military operation that isn't supposed to be occurring, while at the same time Trace goes back to the mainland to talk to the former commander of Special Forces in Vietnam in order to confirm whether or not The Line exists. Boomer barely escapes with his life and comes to the conclusion that a military coup against the President is planned during a practice Command and Control exercise during the President's visit to the Islands.

While Trace meets the commander at the Army-Navy game, Boomer comes into conflict with shadowy military forces on the island of Oahu. Just before the commander is shot, he gives Trace the location of a diary that holds the key to The Line—the only problem is that to recover it, Trace will have to return to West Point. It becomes a race against time, as it appears that The Line will now attack the President at dawn on the 7th at the *Arizona* Memorial as he commemorates the fifty-fourth anniversary of the Japanese attack.

At the last second, the coup is stopped and the major plotters from The Line are killed. But there is still the loose end of the diary and the person close to the President who got Trace and Boomer involved in the first place without their knowledge. Boomer kills the President's man and retrieves the diary. In the end, Boomer and Trace go back to West Point and, in an address to the Corps of Cadets, make public the contents, shredding the veil of secrecy all sides wove.

APPENDIX D: RESOURCES

BOOKS

Agents, Editors and You: The Insider's Guide to Getting Your Book Published, edited by Michelle Howry (Writer's Digest Books). This collection of articles and interviews with industry insiders helps demystify the process of getting published.

Becoming a Writer, by Dorothea Brande and John Gardner (Jeremy P. Tarcher). This classic was originally published in 1934, and offers advice, exercises, and techniques for cultivating the writing life.

The Complete Handbook of Novel Writing, edited by Meg Leder and Jack Heffron (Writer's Digest Books). A series of articles and interviews broken into categories on The Art, The Craft, The Genres, The Marketplace, and so on, giving readers an insider's look at writing and getting published.

The First Five Pages: A Writer's Guide to Staying Out of the Slush Pile, by Noah Lukeman (Fireside). Literary agent Lukeman teaches readers how to identify and avoid bad writing.

How to Write Attention-Grabbing Queries and Cover Letters, by John Wood (Writer's Digest Books). As both writer and editor, Wood brings broad knowledge to this subject and covers magazine queries, as well as fiction and nonfiction book proposals. Also includes samples of queries and cover letters that work and those that don't.

How to Write a Damn Good Novel, by James N. Frey (St. Martin's Press). Basing his instruction on the Three C's—character, conflict, and conclusion—Frey leads readers through writing the novel from the beginning to the end in this informative and authoritative volume.

Novel & Short Story Writer's Market, edited by Anne Bowling (Writer's Digest Books). An annual directory of some 1,900 places to get fiction published, from literary magazines to online markets to book publishers. Also includes listings of conferences and contests, and features instructive articles and interviews with writers and editors.

On Becoming a Novelist, by John Gardner and Raymond Carver (W.W. Norton & Co.). Gardner reflects on his twenty-year career as a novelist, offering the reader insight into what to expect from the work and the writing life. Introduction by Raymond Carver.

The Writer's Digest Writing Clinic, edited by Kelly Nickell (Writer's Digest Books). Instruction on editing your fiction, query letters, and novel synopses. Includes information on joining or forming a critique group.

ORGANIZATIONS

Associated Writing Programs. Sponsors awards, holds an annual conference, and publishes *The Writer's Chronicle* six times a year, which includes essays, articles, news, and information for writers, editors, students, and writing teachers. *The Chronicle* also lists information on grants, awards, fellowships, Web sites, and publishing opportunities. George Mason University, Mailstop 1E3, Fairfax, VA 22030. Tel.: (703) 993-4301. E-mail: awp@gmu.edu. Web site: www.awpwriter.org.

The Authors Guild, Inc. Offers a number of professional services, including a well-organized and experienced contracts department, and seminars on topics such as contract negotiation and publicity. Regular members must have published at least one book or three articles with general circulation periodicals within the last eighteen months; an associate must have a contract for a forthcoming book. Membership benefits include a quarterly journal; e-mail alerts and bulletins; professional seminars; contract services department; group insurance; advocacy on e-rights, copyright, and taxes. 31 E. 28th St., 10th Floor, New York NY, 10016. Tel.: (212) 563-5904. Web site: www.authorsguild.org.

Mystery Writers of America, Inc. Sponsors conferences and presents the Edgar Awards. Membership in MWA is open to published authors, editors, screenwriters, and other professionals in the field. 17 East 47th St., 6th Floor, New York, NY 10017. Tel.: (212) 888-8171. Fax: (212) 888-8107. E-mail: mwa@mysterywriters.org. Web site: www.mysterywriters.org.

Romance Writers of America. Provides market and craft information at the national level; chapters provide support and mentoring to writers in the same geographical area or those working in the same subgenre. Membership benefits include newsletter; annual conference; e-mail lists and bulletins; professional seminars; contests and awards; mentoring; publisher and agent lists. 3707 FM 1960 W., Suite 555, Houston TX 77068. Tel.: (281) 440-6885. Web site: www.rwanational.org.

Science Fiction and Fantasy Writers of America, Inc. An organization for science fiction and fantasy writers, artists, editors, and other professionals. Membership benefits include conference; awards; magazines; insurance; grievance committee; bulletin; handbooks. P.O. Box 877, Chestertown, MD 21620 Web site: www.sfwa.org.

Sisters in Crime. Promotes women mystery writers. Membership benefits include newsletter; publications; support of special interest groups, minorities, and new writers. Box 442124, Lawrence KS 66044-8933. Tel.: (785) 842-1325. Web site: www.sistersincrime.org.

Western Writers of America. Promotes the literature of the American West, sponsors an annual convention, and presents Spur Awards. Members include traditional western fiction writers, as well as historians and other nonfiction authors, young adult and romance writers, and writers interested in regional history. 1012 Fair St., Franklin TN 37064-2718. Tel.: (615) 791-1444. Web site: www.westernwriters.org.

APPENDIX E: SAMPLE STORY GRID

Chapter	Start Page	End Page	Date/Day	Local Time
Prologue	1	12	12/21/71	8:20 A.M.
				5:30 P.M.
1	13	27	11/22/93	2:30 P.M.
			Monday	4:00 P.M.
2	28	41	11/23/93	8:30 A.M.
			Tuesday	11:45 A.M.
3	42	61	11/24/93	10:43 A.M.
			Wednesday	11:00 A.M.
4	62	74		4:00 P.M.
5	75	89	11/25/93	8:41 A.M.
			Thursday	9:00 A.M.
6	90	102		1:12 P.M.
				12:52 P.M.
				6:00 P.M.

Zulu/Greenwich Mean Time	Location/Setting	Action: a brief summary of what happens
20/2120	Antartica	Plane leaves site/crashes
21/0300	CO	Get call
22/1830	NPRC	Sam finds photos
22/2000	NPRC	Tracks/goes home
23/1430	NPRC	To RC-PAC
23/1745	NPRC	Learn it's Antartica
24/1543	SNN	Ben makes calls
24/1700	NPRC	Sam finds aircrew data
24/2200	SNN	Sam gets permission
25/1341	Boston	Intro Brackman
25/1400	SNN	Ben calls sister/itinerary
25/1812	SNN	Meeting
25/1853	NPRC	Zerox pictures
25/2300	NY	UN official sees report

APPENDIX F: SAMPLE PLOT LINE

Time	Harmon	Araki
Wed. 8 Oct.	Lake	
9:30 A.M.	Lake's story Realize it's SF	
11:30 A.M.	Word on NK ships	
12:15 P.M.	Harbor info, on sub Feliks calls	
1:00 P.M.	Meet Araki	Get info, on sub Made it!

Kuzumi	Nishin	Feliks	Misc.
Realize forest is SF			
	Get info; kill Jonas		
	Go to yakuza w/no.	Calls Lake	
	Lake apartment	I'm coming	
	Yakuza shows up	Jonas/Tunnel	
Get Nishin info.	Find him		
Get Araki info.	Trawler info./help		

INDEX